Jock's Journey

memoir of a minister and makar

Jock Stein

British Library Cataloguing in Publication Data:
a catalogue record for this publication
is available from the British Library

ISBN   978-1-912052-46-2

Typeset in 11pt Minion Pro at Haddington, Scotland

Print and cover design by West Port Print & Design,
St Andrews

Contents

For my children and grand-children,
who are living their own stories,
and my dear wife Margaret
who has not only illustrated this book
but graced my life for 50 years

Noddfa is a retreat centre in Wales where Margaret did this drawing

MY THANKS

to Brenda Lealman and Roger Garfitt:
  you got me started writing serious poetry.
to Rachel Cadell, widow of my friend and cousin Patrick:
  you encouraged me to go ahead with this.
to four much better writers who very kindly read the book
  and commended it:
  Irene Howat, John Miller, James Robertson, Catherine Simpson
– part of the legion of wonderful people whose paths crossed mine,
  only some of whom are mentioned here.

INTRODUCTION

A memoir is a vanity project, although I have published memoirs for other people which were not like that. But usually it is, at least in part. You choose what you want to say, and hope readers will enjoy it. A memoir is not a biography where the writer explores a character in depth, and in the process may cause some hurt to the subject and to other people. I have tried not to do that, and simply enjoyed the writing – even if there are many others more deserving of a memoir. Both memoirs and biographies, however, make you vulnerable, perhaps in different ways. A memoir also gives me the opportunity to express my gratitude to some of the people who have blessed my life, not least my wife and family, and to the God I have come to know and love.

I also wondered about giving this book the title 'Anglo-Scot'. Dangerous. It has many meanings, like a Scot living in England, or an English person living in Scotland, or a Scot who is a closet (or an open) Unionist, or . . . it gets muddier. However, I am none of these. I am a Scot who loves England and the English as well as Scotland and the Scots. I play the bagpipes. I have published poetry in Scots. I have voted for the SNP, but not all the time. And whatever your politics, the 'social union' of Scotland and England will endure.

It was Hugh MacDiarmid who spoke about being 'whaur extremes meet'. Sometimes I have been around when something like this was happening. If you were simply to read the first few chapters, you might never guess that I had a bit part in, for example:

- a conversation between Donald Dewar and Alex Salmond that led to one of the rare times when Scottish Labour and the SNP worked together . . .

- a conversation with Tom Nairn in which he rescinded his famous remark that Scotland would never be free until the last minister had been strangled with the last copy of the Sunday Post . . .

- a conversation between Christians and Muslims on different approaches to banking . . .

- a conversation between the internationally famous Christian leaders John Stott and John Wimber which would surprise those who remember what both men stood for . . .

- a conversation with Cardinal Suenens about ecumenism and a conversation with the head of the Benedictine Order in Hungary about the Pope . . .

I would love to say I was there when Ian Paisley and Martin McGuinness learned to have a conversation, but it would be untrue. I do recommend the DVD called 'The Journey', about that. My journey is more modest – but is the journey of any human being really modest? The answer of people of any and every religion, I suspect, would be a firm 'no'.

Where the search for truth is concerned, the philosopher Plato considered poets to be not colleagues, but rivals. I disagree. So, I have included a lot of poetry in this book. Since everyone is a philosopher in some sense, searching for wisdom, I hope that what I write will shed light rather than heat on the issues of our time, and suggest that many extremes may be simply different peaks on the same mountain range.

Coming back to sea level, in the life of people and nations, it sometimes seems as though the tide has gone out leaving us stuck on sandbanks. If nothing else, that gives us time to greet each other as friends, as this sonnet written in Wales suggests.

The Dyfi Estuary Ampersand

Now you see it, now you don't,
but now's the time the river takes a breath,
its energy passed out to sea,
Welsh dragon fire extinguished at low tide.
Here sandbanks rise, unfurl their necks
with golden curls, to make an ampersand
that calls each river bank to raise
a hand and greet the other. Sand formations
mirror clouds which lift and drift,
bind earth and sky, remind us that a high tide
cannot shift the low behind,
each ampersand a stealthy strand of DNA.

What is submerged when life is in full flow
will rise when dry times come, and ask, "And so?"

Chapter One

GROWING UP

I was a late entrant, arriving in winter 1941 just when my parents had given up hope of any children. And I'm still late; writing this in the fourth quarter of my one and only century. Scotland has seen plenty of these snatches of time, and I'm about to do my share of picking up pieces of her past and present, her places, her people, her politics. But first a poem about my mother.

Around

She had a birthday yesterday –
past her century, she would be:
matter of fact, picking blackcurrants
just the other side of the bush.
She'll prefer to bottle them, the old way,
and then she'll want news of the children.
I'm glad she's around today,
though she may not eat with us.
That final week, the way she figured it,
her time had come; and food was in the past.
She never let the pan boil over.
She was always in charge.

Dorothea Cadell (her maiden name) was almost 90 when she decided it was time to go, and not be a burden on the family. So she stopped eating. I cared for her in that final week, with a nurse coming in at night, and it was at night she died – I think, being a private person, she wanted it that way.

I never wrote poetry while she was alive. I guess I troubled her with enough things without adding that. Though she did have her share of the arts in her family – Jean Cadell was an actress, her cousin Bunty is now known as the famous Scottish Colourist F.C.B. Cadell, and somewhere I have a wee book of watercolours she painted out in Palestine looking after nephews and nieces following the First War. Her brother-in-law Robin Elsdale was an engineer working with the army under the British Mandate.

1

She also worked as matron at a small school in Stow, in the Scottish Borders. We still have a silver pair of tweezers, shaped like a stork, which she was given by the School Governors because she discovered a fire which had started in the boarding house, and got all the children safely out.

I always assumed they were scissors till my wife Margaret started to draw them, as the bill opens and closes just like a pair of scissors. I think  of two scissor blades as a model of two different, but equally sharp features being harnessed to good effect, and made to work together. A model of a good marriage perhaps. It describes what I remember of my own parents' relationship.

My mother's own gifts included hospitality, making people welcome, and providing quantities of food, grown and bottled, not least during the Second War. She kept hens, and my first memories were at that level, hearing them clucking, picking eggs out of dirty straw. But I can just recall seeing the searchlights chasing enemy aircraft over Grangemouth at night. A stronger memory is of being in the Falkirk Royal Infirmary a year after the War – a miserable week. (Just before the hospital closed around 2010 I noticed my father's name on a board as a donor – his obituary notice says he was the hospital chairman.)

Tonsilitis, 1946

I have blanked out the hard memories,
thrust them through the trapdoor
into a dark world of terrible things,
icy heads floating in a silent sea,
breathy beasts snuffling at my throat,
insects crawling, crawling towards me.
I remember only the absence of home
and a mother forbidden to visit.

My mother was known as Da, and the second youngest. Big families in those days – she was the seventh child, and if I had been also seventh I could have expected the second sight. As it was, she married my father Alan Stein after his first wife died having her third child Sheila; Alan knew her already, since they rode to hounds together, and as my mother once said, "We both knew what we wanted." There were two older children for her to look after as well, Maisie and Alan.

Hunting was on a Saturday. My father also took time off on a Sunday afternoon to play bridge with the Stevensons at Polmont Park, another of the 'big houses' which are now all gone. I can remember being carried in as an infant to the room where they were playing. When I was about seven I heard a saying of Mr Stevenson quoted, "The cards never forgive" – in other words, if you play a good hand badly, you can say goodbye to the thought of getting any other good hands. It was my first introduction to the idea of fate, and my lifelong interest in the tension between fate (however understood) and freewill.

One of the perks of a Memoir is the ability to dodge about. At this point I need another poem to put in so that you will be able to read the three following poems without going over a page, and seventy years on, I can't resist reminding you that Scotland is not fated to lose to England at Twickenham. This poem is actually about Psalm 126, "When the Lord restored the fortunes of Zion, we were like those who dream."

> *That game we drew*
> *at Twickenham,*
> *all fifteen players*
> *heroes, legends;*
> *divine catchup,*
> *return from exile.*
>
> *You did it once,*
> *now do it again,*
> *God of surprises.*

> *Do it for Scotland,*
> *do it for England,*
> *do it for everyone*
> *and every people*
> *who set out*
> *on pilgrimage.*

There is a connection with my mother, who years later suddenly decided that none of her family were interested in rugby, and (without consultation) sold her debenture which gave us two seats at Murrayfield for every match. But I am getting away ahead of the game . . .

After they married, my parents had to wait ten years before I came along, Da busy all the time with the three older children. My Sunday name is John. What happened was this. A few months after me, my cousin John was born – and my own father was so annoyed about confusion of names among those likely to run the family business in future, that I was from that moment on always called Jock.

This ten year gap meant that my own childhood, while outwardly full and happy, was also a bit lonely. Albert Einstein once said, "I live in that solitude which is painful in youth, but delicious in the years of maturity."

Sounds of Childhood

That strong gong calls me down to eat,
see the soft smack of my old half-sister
greet her father with a formal kiss.
The days are easy, full of the futt and putt
of ancient tennis balls, the whirr of a grouse
disturbed, the fright of someone else's gun.

Closer, the hummer of a pony's greeting,
his gentle proo to clear his cavities,
that solid clock on cobbles after I have
lifted fetlock to pick out a hoof.

What about the whizz of air, as you speed
too fast downhill, clutching handlebars?
The rush of snow beneath your old toboggan
as you brake before that graveyard of a burn?

Billiard balls go clack, but snooker cluck
– in memory at least; the games we share,
like billiard fives, or slosh or billiard football:
wild enough, but always condescending.

When the tennis court becomes a dance floor
late at night, and I am locked in bed,
too young to join her 21st, her party night,
I hear the music of the ceilidh band,
I watch the whirl and fling of far off kilts,
but feel the silence of an only child.

My sister Sheila kept up her love of horses and rural life, married a farmer, John Dudgeon – who became Master of the Linlithgow and Stirlingshire Hunt at a time when fox-hunting was an accepted part of country life – and continued riding in point to point races. I remember parties at Callendar House, home of Colonel Forbes, a previous Master of the Hunt – in common with many of those great houses, this 14th century mansion is now a gallery and events centre, and run by the Falkirk Community Trust.

Like many boys, I was more into activities than relationships. A natural one was riding, as we kept horses, and my first pony was called Donald – a slow beast, whose size reminded me that I was at the bottom of the family, even when Maisie and Alan had left home, since parents and Sheila had horses, not ponies. I would in due course learn how to do dressage, pass Pony Club exams – but I never fell in love with horses.

I nearly joined the local gang in Old Polmont. They half-welcomed me, gave me a crude nickname I was then too young to understand, but that was enough for my parents to divert my friendships south, to the neighbouring village of Brightons. Most of my friends since have been from the south, except my wife Margaret who is a northerner.

I was not brought up an 'Anglo-Scot'. The word was not used. In those days rivalries between Edinburgh and Glasgow, or indeed between one gang and another, were more important than wider rivalries. The war of 1939-45 had not wiped out nationalities, but it melded people together, and the dominance of Labour and Tory Governments ensured that unionism was the unspoken background to life.

After the war, priorities were rebuilding after survival. Heavy industry, fishing and farming were the main sources of Scottish livelihood. Harvest was a great social occasion for children, when technology was only just beginning to overturn the rationing of progress during the early post-war years.

Remember the Harvest

Stooks took forks to prong and pitch
with practised hips;
bales are spat out with no taste
of barley on the lips
which open to release a ton
of straw with certainly
no room to breathe like sheaves. It leaves
a lot to be desired,
like harvest picnics, tail boards sat upon
by children, pulled by
early tractors, unprofessional machines
between the combine and the horse.

That poor, pent, post-war period,
rationed, spent remembering a culture
rich at heart and hairst.

It was also the period of railways, before Dr Beeching wielded his axe. My best friend Peter Meadows lived just over Polmont Station, where his father was stationmaster. Those were the days when engine names were common and collectable, my favourite being the small locomotives which boasted a wide range of characters from the Waverley novels. Walter Scott, of course, is now described as an Anglo-Scot, even though he was more ardent a Scot than that unionist poet Robert Burns.

Girl on a Train

*Brown hair drops around her profile, flanks
her secrets under that yellow jacket.*
Beyond,

*the Ochils keep their counsel at a distance,
while the train slips easily into a cutting,
scattering quick eye sips of March primrose,
hints of daffodil.*
The girl sits still,

*studies her iphone, fingers the Pullman table,
starts to fold up every scrap of ticket,
swings her rucsac on her yellow back,
stands, turns for the door,*
gets out at Polmont.

*Sixty years ago I watched these trains:
hoarded every scrap of time to cycle
to my friend's house, get a grandstand view.
We leaned across the station master's wall
to note the engine names*
like Quentin Durward

carved in steel, and notch up engine numbers.

*A boy on the platform eyes her jacket,
conjectures a brave yell, 'Hello',
imagines he has got her number.*

That boy was a lot older than I was then. It's hard for modern teenagers to realise how innocent we were, before television, before social media. Well, not quite before television: I remember how my father would have nothing to do with it until, suddenly, a set appeared for the Queen's coronation in 1953.

Things remained local and media-free all through my boarding school years, which began at Clifton Hall, near Newbridge. Before that my education combined disaster and privilege; disaster when I was taken one morning to Calstock Primary School on the east side of Falkirk, where I threw a tantrum, howled and howled until I was removed and taken home; was that terror, or manipulation, or both? Privilege when I joined my cousins Patrick and Jimmie Cadell, and two other children, to be taught by the redoubtable Miss Baillie in Linlithgow. There I never howled. It would not have occurred to me, or to Miss Rhoda Baillie, that such behaviour was possible in her presence. I confuse her now in memory with Miss Jean Brodie, although Miss Baillie would have been outraged by the comparison.

From Clifton Hall I got a music scholarship to Sedbergh – not too hard, my playing of a piece by J.S. Bach seemed to do the trick; all I can remember is the melody . . . My headmaster, Richard Killick, drove me down to Yorkshire, then its home county, and drove me back, partly (I realised later) because my father had just died at home, and I was being kept in careful ignorance till the exam was over. He was extremely kind. My father's death was of course a shock, as was the decision by the Killick family to invite me some years later to take my headmaster's funeral – the first I ever took, while still a student. But I never questioned the way things happened – few of us did in those days.

Fathers

My father had a good war, so they said,
and lucky, a bullet passing through his chest;
close to comrades, and to later colleagues
in the firm, all those who knew him best.

I saw him lying, pale and dying, just before
the new term started at my boarding school.
My nursing aunt soon shooed me out the door;
they kept me kindly absent from the funeral.

Headmaster acted father for a while,
hard schooled me in the interim,
let my comrade chums hold my morale,
and set me fair to prosper in the firm.

This stand in father died a few years later –
no church connection, better not to make it
too religious. I was still a student . . . just
a family funeral . . . they asked me to take it.

The First War, where my father was decorated for bravery in action, and was wounded three times, had a massive effect on Britain, and

Scotland in particular, where we lost proportionately more young men, although it was much worse in the rural areas (Selkirk was hard hit losing over 20% of their young men, Lewis lost an incredible 20% of their whole population); the shipbuilders and steelmakers of the industrial West made sure they retained most of their workforce under the guise of 'essential war work'. A century later, I was to publish a book of poems in Scots and English by Irene Howat called *The Crackit Cup*, a moving description of how that War impacted an Ayrshire village.

Afterwards, like many of his contemporaries, my father was an agnostic or an atheist, though I was never old enough to discuss that with him; but of course he still supported the activities of the local church at Polmont where my mother was a member.

He commanded the 7th Battalion of the Argyll and Sutherland Highlanders after the War, was given the rank of Brevet Colonel in 1924, and chaired the Stirlingshire Territorial Army and Air Force Association from 1925; during the Second War he was in what was later called 'Dad's Army'. One of his close friends was Ralph Risk, who also earned a Military Cross and bar, became a solicitor in Maclay, Murray and Spens and the family lawyer, and a good friend to me after my father died when I was only 12.

My father was a hard driver. I cannot resist including this satirical poem about him, written by 'J.G.' at Gully Post, near Gavrelle, Arras in June 1918. It was passed on by John Clark, father-in law of my second cousin Emily Sanderson; a friend of his had discovered it among the papers of his own father, who had possibly served with my father, then Major Alan Stein, in the Argylls.

When the summer days are fine
an' we're tourin' up the line,
an' tae hae an easy time we're unco keen,
that's the time we get the knock
wi' a maist alarmin' shock
frae oor brainy work controller – MAJOR STEIN

For it's Stein, Stein, Stein,
sic a man has never been,
a man sae fu' o' work I've never seen.
I could nearly bet a fiver
that ye served, as a slave-driver
in the auld days when they ca'd ye "MISTER STEIN"

Ye've been never known tae shirk
when it comes tae makin' work,
an the boys a' want tae ken jist what ye mean,
humpin' shovels or barbed wire
till they bloomin' near expire,
but you never seem to tire – MAJOR STEIN

For it's Stein, Stein, Stein
you're the hottest stuff I've seen,
for the men ye dinna care a horse's bean;
ye jist watch them wi' a smile
diggin' trenches by the mile,
it jist seems tae be your style – MAJOR STEIN.

Dae ye never tak' a thocht
o' the havoc ye hae wrocht
wi' the tempers o' the men – it's plainly seen.
But I doot there'll come a day
when ye'll rue the awfu' way
ye hae treated freemen born – MAJOR STEIN

For it's Stein, Stein, Stein
in the past whate'er ye've been,
tak a tummle tae yersel and cut it clean,
or some boy that's oot for fun
wi' his wee bit service gun
Micht jist stop ye on the run – MAJOR STEIN!

He was also very fair. I came across a talk given by the Revd W. Jardine in Wallace Green Church, Berwick, in 1920 which mentions how Major Alan Stein in the late summer of 1918 was repelling a German attack. By his side was a private who proved a hero. His commanding officer wanted to recommend him for a decoration – but the man had disappeared; my father would not let any recommendation go forward for himself until the fellow was found. Months later, after the Armistice, Mr Jardine came across a wounded soldier billeted in a town in Belgium and gave him some grapes which 'the Major' had given him. "The Major is a fine gentleman," he said, "and he spoke very kind to me in the bombing raid at Gavrelle." So the man finally got his D.C.M.

Some great poets emerged out of that First War; here are two short poems of my own from the Second War, recognising how lucky my generation has been compared with those before and after. The first is a cinquain (two, four, six, eight and two syllables) and the second a tercet.

War and Peace

They paid
the wartime bill
and so we owe them, though
we make our children shoulder all
the debt.

War Babies

Two thousand and fifteen: platinum jubilee
for the war end babies, born
to somehow drive this life-long spree

of growth from rationing to plenty,
from keeping hens and shooting game
to supermarket trollies, seventy

years to run down social capital,
abandon post-war certainties,
watch their sons and grandsons whittle

inheritance down to the brittle bones,
Parties govern by referenda,
children live on mobile phones.

In front a promised land may lie
– or maybe not – but either way
most in the wilderness will die.

That's all about transition. It's a bit bleak, and I have to ask myself, is this the pessimism of old age, or is it a wise judgment on our age? Is the bottle half full or half empty? Is it our faster awareness of human tragedy through the media? Is it our inability to cope with the transfer of world power and leadership to China and India?

But at this stage I was learning to cope with a new school. I have a copy (typed – his handwriting was illegible) of a letter my father sent to Mr Killick in December 1953 making it quite clear that at age twelve I should be working towards a BSc at Cambridge! Accordingly, I had already given up classics, at which I excelled (thanks to Mr Killick) in favour of science, at which I was mediocre; I still remember the ignominy of seeing 'Stein's Circuit' chalked up on the blackboard as a warning to others of how not to wire an electrical circuit. In the end, I scraped an entry to Emmanuel College, Cambridge, by dint of a 'general scholarship examination' which included French and English, for which I had managed to get a school prize.

Holidays are extra special for those at boarding school, and summer had the bonus of Boat of Garten, where we had been going since I was age 4, staying initially in the Boat Hotel and latterly in Street of Kincardine. It was there that I first met John Miller, who would in due course become one of the Church of Scotland Assembly Moderators, and very recently the editor of *Finding the Way*, a book the Handsel Press published just a few years ago, featuring the remarkable Czech pastor and former dissident, Tomas Bisek.

However my greatest challenge and delight during these years was learning to read the Bible as a living book; that happened entirely due to a discovery of God, during a Scripture Union holiday at the Gean House in Alloa. The following poem describes what happened.

Changes

Let's style it black and white to colour,
flash into an unforeseen dimension,
without drugs or mania or magic;
just the staying power of what
a prisoner penned 2000 years ago:
"Behold, I stand at the door and knock;
if anyone listen, hear my voice, and open,
I will come in and share that life."

Such changes happen in unlikely places,
with all kinds of motives; and what better
reason makes a teenager rebel than when
a wiser friend comes in to stay, and say
"It's time to go another way; keep faith,
then you and I will work it out together".

'Friend' is not a bad word to describe
what later study would declare as 'Father,
Son and Holy Spirit'; God welcomes equally
the learned, and the simple, trusting child.

After some time, news of this filtered through to my cousins who were running the family business, which was making firebricks and other refractory products. Colin Stein in particular was sceptical, and gave me a hard time, asking me what I would do when selling in the Eastern

European market where customers expected perks like prostitutes. I couldn't give him a good answer, but the collapse of the refractories industry would in due course take us all out of that scene; the time was coming when changes in the steel industry would mean that one firebrick was required where ten had been previously.

What made faith stick was the Bible. I had tried reading it once at my primary school (called 'prep school'), and soon got bored. Now I started again, and came across Jesus saying 'forgive your enemies'. I had made plenty at school, guys I loathed, so I thought, 'Better see how this works out'. To my surprise, when I changed my attitude and stopped slagging them off, the others changed too, quite dramatically. That wouldn't convince a sceptic, but it convinced a teenager like me. I gave up swearing – but nothing I ever heard subsequently came as a surprise to my ears; at boarding school you knew all the language, even if only a very few were practitioners.

I enjoyed singing choruses which today are dismissed as hopelessly old-fashioned, but are simple and to the point, and this one encouraged me to stay on this radical new track:

> *Keep me humble Lord, keep me shining Lord, in all I say and do*
> *That the world may see Christ lives in me and learn to love him too.*

Back home, my sheltered life including a lot of music making, some with my Cadell cousins at Grange in Linlithgow, where I learned to drink tea without sugar simply because it was assumed there that no right-minded person needed sugar – half a century before the modern preoccupation with reducing sugar intake.

Although my own instrument was the piano, shortly to be extended to bagpipes, the instrument I revered was the violin, and my favourite book Robert Magidoff's early biography of Yehudi Menuhin.

The Violin Concerto

He was a god
who flashed his feathered wings
for Felix Mendelssohn, for Alexander Gibson,
for the boy perched cheaply in the upper tier,
half-ready and half-formed.

His teenage years
saw Menuhin go back to basics,
work his muscles, stance and fluid brain
into his gifts as prodigy, all things
re-shaped, re-formed.

So man and music
filled the Usher Hall that night,
and cast a horoscope with strings
of melody and magic, and a boy
transfixed, transformed.

Sedbergh School, for a boy who had recently lost his father, was a gift. Many of the boys were Scots, often farmers' sons from the Scottish borders. Provided you could survive the first year, in those days much tougher with fagging and cold baths than it is today, a world of learning, music and sport soon wrapped itself around you. It was, as the school motto proclaimed, *dura virum nutrix* – a hard mother of men – but I loved the hills and I accepted the discipline, living in Sedgwick House.

Some like my friend Peter Mawby developed special interests like bird-watching. His father was in charge of Winder House, which is why he landed up in Sedgwick. Close by was the famous Quaker Meeting House at Brigflatts, final home of the poet Basil Bunting (who spelt his epic poem Briggflatts with an extra g). It was only a mile from Sedbergh, but it would be sixty years before I visited it. For me, formal religion was the weekly chapel service and my first encounter with George MacLeod, the legendary leader of the Iona Community, who presided at my confirmation.

In those days it was assumed that Scots would be confirmed into the Church of Scotland, and everybody else into the Church of England. Beforehand, MacLeod interviewed us, and asked us a question, "What is your image of God?" – no doubt expecting us to talk about an old man with a white beard, and be suitably corrected. To my credit, or shame, I smugly told him that "God was Spirit, and those who worship must worship in spirit and truth" (quoting John's Gospel).

It was at Sedbergh that I had my first sense of call to be a minister. The school chaplain was preaching, an otherworldly character whom we all made fun of, but the sermon challenged me. My reaction was one of mild horror – this guy is such a wimp it can't be him, it must be God speaking to me! This was followed, sensibly I think, by the thought that Jesus was 30 before he began his life's ministry, and I ought to get some experience of life before I considered anything so daft or dramatic as becoming a minister.

Anyhow, I continue to enjoy climbing the fells around the school, and at home the nearby Ochils. In those days, with minimal road traffic, we could reach them on bicycles; there was only one piece of dual carriageway, between Skinflats and the Kincardine Bridge. Some say 'Skinflats' comes from an old Dutch word for 'good' (*schoen*) and 'flats', the name bestowed by Dutch engineers working on land reclamation in the 17th century, but it may be Scots in origin.

I wasn't much into poetry as a boy, though I have spotted one poem in the school magazine (*The Phoenix*) which I co-edited, but I recall writing a couplet which, while of little value as poetry, did express my feelings at the time:

Eyes upon the mountains, solid, vast,
Waiting till the guiding glen is cut at last.

I met some interesting characters through getting involved in camps run by Scripture Union, where I later served as quartermaster. George Martin and Peter Barclay-Watt are still friends today. Hamish Brown was another, later famous for writing *Hamish's Mountain Walk*. Hamish encouraged us to walk (and run) over the Ochils with bare feet, a habit which I also took back to Sedbergh, whose fells are grassy like these hills. Remembering that time led to the following poem.

Barefoot

Barefoot, brazen, feel the pulse
which carries you across the hills.
Make those tendons trample
on your tendency
to keep things nicely shod
in paragraphs . . .

Feel the ground you take for granted,
touch the grass you seldom notice,
wrap your toes around the unseen foothills
making every track unique.
Then stride. Spread out your wings
and touch the sky.

Now beat them, spin the axes
that define our three dimensions,
write the flight path of this strange,
strong human being
that runs barefoot, brazen, all across
the Ochil hills.

I wrote another later poem featuring the Ochils, looking out of a window in Crieff Hydro at wreaths of fog along the north side of the hills. This poem was not about myself but about Scotland as it was in the early years of devolution.

Cloud and Fire

Surreal winter cloudscape, three times layered
along the Ochils, cradling Sherriffmuir
as if to gentle history, and make
an overture in art to things impossible.

Take time and outstretched fingers, run them
carefully along those bars of fog, soft striped
dawnwear for the hills which know the time
to sleep, and wake when Spring unfolds, to
do the duty of each season; or maybe
veils, concealing futures languishing
in jails, unvisited since unimagined?
What season now for Scotland, what videotype
of land is waiting to be brought to birth?
Stylish, connected, rich in mind – or just unkind?

What poet politician is there who will dare
lift off the blindfolds we all wear
and speak the words we cannot say?
What fire by night will match the cloud by day?

In those days I had no interest in politics. It was never discussed either at home or school. The British Empire was about to fold, before long Tom Nairn would write his book *The Break-Up of Britain*, but I was blissfully uninterested in such things. My wider thoughts, when not occupied with helping with boys' camps outwith school, were confined to career prospects, and every so often to the thought that it would be nice to have a girl friend.

I was expected to take over the family business, which unknown to me was about to hit the storms of technological and political change which would in the end sink all the heavy industry in Central Scotland. But at this point John G. Stein and Co. Ltd was still an independent world leader, and family power undiminished. While I had not forgotten that challenge to become a minister, I was trying to focus on the science which would let me get a job with one of our customers in the steel industry.

For those who had some talent, public schools offered much. I had the chance to perform the last movement of Beethoven's First Piano Concerto with the school orchestra (by far the easiest of his concertos). And we took for granted the sight-singing of madrigals, conducting groups and arranging music. Privilege indeed, though at least we were well told that it was now our task to serve those less privileged.

I also remember playing the organ for a small part of Handsel's Messiah. Accompanying the choruses is demanding; I recall occasionally looking in the mirror beside the organ and realising that the conductor was having to follow me rather than the other way around – and reflecting perhaps for the first time on whether the exercise of such power is good or bad, and whether one has much choice in the matter, as much of life is simply about duty and survival.

I enjoyed running over the fells, did the local 'three peaks' (Whernside, Ingleborough and Pen-y-Ghent), and would later do the bigger three, Ben Nevis, Scafell Pike and Snowdon in about 22 hours – not bad for the days before motorways. My love of the high ground was however focused on the Cairngorms. Years later I would remember those days, and write about the magic and mystery of these mountains.

High Poetry

(with thanks to Ásta Fanney Sigurðardóttir and StAnza 2017)

Cairngorm grit scrunches under my boots,
provoking the quiet scuffle of ptarmigan
somewhere in the mist towards MacDhui. Bent
under a rucsac of questions, I hear no mention
of grey men (or women); now the mountain

draws its granite curtains round my soul,
wraps me in a weird eternity, where sense
is scrambled, shuffled into one day's journey,
flanking carefully the snow-lipped corrie,
on to the Lurcher's Crag, down into the Lairig.

I have pulled out some words, left them behind me
to interrogate the peaks all hidden in the cloud,
those markers of long time, white-capped, grey-gowned,
scoured by the cut and thrust of seething magma
forty million years ago; a serious timescale,
if one day's a thousand years, and space-time bends
around eternal purpose, weird and wonderful;
or is it only we who feel the wind, and bend,
and try to make a nest inside the hurricane?

Walking is forgetting to remember anything
except a map, a compass and a bivvy bag.
Climbing is remembering your comfort zone
but wanting to expand it. Journeys take us,
break us open to fiaski, middle distance,
risky, liminal space that turns hills blue.
Words pass through grit and grey, dance off
a grand chain with some misty faith posts,
straighten up our poetry to human height,
eternity a scree run for another day.

The other hills which entranced me were those around Loch Duich, in the West Highlands. I was introduced to this part of the world by my Cadell cousins, who regularly spent summer holidays there, and once took me to the Falls of Glomach in the pouring rain; I discovered that this was a ritual also imposed on any would-be suitor for their older sister Helen, and the wetter the weather the more likely that such a young man might be suitable if he survived the day out.

At Inverinate, my mother and I used to stay in a cottage called 'The Knoll', tucked under an eponymous hillock, but with a view of the loch from an upper window. I must have already been stubborn in those days: on one occasion we had been cutting peat some way up a hill, and a pile was left to be collected another day. By this time I had what I later admitted was 'flu, but I insisted on going back up the hill, filling two sacks with peat and coming down with them balanced on a pole across the back of my neck.

That led to a spell in bed with pneumonia. I remember the rain and the frustration, not least because it was entirely my own fault.

Autumn Rain

I can see the loch
at the corner of the window.
The loch is dull, grey, gull-grey,
fuller now, not far away
and Noah is watching it too,
arms akimbo, frowning at the rain:
builder's arms, grimed, hairs heavy
with the touch of pitch.

I can see the loch
in the corner of my mind,
the boat bobbing a little,
wondering why I do not come.
I haul the net of my thoughts
out of the water, across the grass,
round the knoll to the front door,
pull it inside. Winter is coming.

Noah is bored, looking at the loch
growing, stretching out
far beyond the kyle.
Time has been submerged
with the hills and the roads,
and I am sailing with him
on a sea of error, failings
and this well-deserved pneumonia.

'Do lung scars last for ever?'
I asked Noah. He opened a window,
smelt the flesh dead in the water.
What does he hear, as the sea
spills over one last island, kills
a last lament? He said,
'There is the rumour of a rainbow.'
Should I listen to rumours?

Happily, the scars healed, and the drama of the poem faded along with my adolescence. The rumour of university was about to become reality – but not before what nowadays would be called a gap year.

Chapter Two

IONA and INDUSTRY

It took me a while to get to Iona. When I left Sedbergh in 1959 it was to fly out to Christchurch, in New Zealand, stopping *en route* in Iran and Singapore, where we spent time in the Raffles Hotel while the plane got fixed. I had a night in Sydney, where the temperature was over 40° (108° Fahrenheit in those days, which was seriously warm).

Air travel was something of a novelty. Nowadays we are more practised and more cynical, not least because of the escalating rounds of security. This poem was written in Malta Airport in 2012.

Air Travel

Travellers and their hand held bits now pass
in pulses through security, essential hourglass,
then settle with relief or something stronger
round the buffet. Departure queues grow longer
at the gates, as up to date procedures level
down the quality of flying. So, what devil
in the legislative detail causes so much checking
in and out? Perhaps we're wired for wrecking
every chance we get to live more simply. Trust
has flown, and now our masters must
just bite these boring bullets, and accept
the consequence of faith so badly kept.

Life in 1960 was still relatively simple. Outside Christchurch I worked on a farm. I would like to say that I entered into dialogue with another culture – what I remember is 'heading' peas with a combine, and sitting up a tree eating apricots. After travelling round the South Island I spent time with relatives in the North, before flying on to Washington DC and then New York. I was in a hurry to get home to Scotland, where I was due to help with a boys' camp at Easter Time.

It was a very Presbyterian attitude to life, though I didn't know that at the time. Much later, I would visit a Retreat Centre called Los Olivos in the

Sierra Nevada Mountains, and find myself entranced by the ants and their industry, which allowed me to add a bit of poetry to the dour Presbyterian attitude to working life.

A Proverb Reconsidered

Tracking wild across the Sierra Nevada,
the ants are in God's eye, a little armada
of twitching purpose, joyfully numbered,
since one ant is worth a thousand elephants
in heaven's economy. Even one dumb bird
is not an oxymoron, and God (for instance)
puts a single anthill on the same sure
footing as a skyscraper, because they share
the solid earth, and need the same pure
air. With God one single petal is as fair
as any grand bouquet, two millimetres
rank beside two thousand metres.

How to recalibrate our thought
is something urgent that we ought
to do. For if an insignificant ant
can ferry something twenty times its size
with giant energy, keep constant
witness to God's algebra, surprise
us all with tricks of geo-engineering,
then we need to get down on our knees
and see through God's own lens, peering
at these little creatures and their cities,
nests of enterprise; for God is adamant,
and tells us slugs, "Observe the ant!"

I had studied advanced maths at school, but with little enthusiasm. Even when my wife succumbed to sudoku, in practice I stuck carefully to crosswords, having lost any taste I ever had for numbers.

Numbers

Numbers, I hate them.
They crawl like half-dead wasps
into the corridors of every day life.
I won't touch them, they might sting
me into filling in a questionnaire;
they might creep over my wrist
and die somewhere in my sleeve;
then I would be responsible for
death certificates, reasons
why Bernoulli's model fails, and
all the facts of prospect theory.

Let numbers stay unborn, imaginary,
nested in some virtual algorithm
where some boffins get a buzz.

Even sudoku I am suspicious of today. I would like to describe what follows as a love poem, if somewhat back-handed.

Premeditation

She turns towards me, but already I have risen,
ready for the writing. In late sleep she snuffles,
sinuses less sinuous than once. She is rejuvenating
from another day spent tirelessly for others,
with the only break her midnight tryst
with a square faced lover, waiting patiently
to feel her hand caress and summon him
from folded sleep inside her handbag.

However, things are not between them as they were;
Sudoku Sid is difficult; no longer strictly logical;
his questions make her guess, and even worry.
So I fear this dear relationship is breaking up,
and while another man might welcome such an end
to blatant double timing, what I dread is there
inside her head, and even now she's poised to touch
his geeky brother, as he lurks within her mobile,
smirking, fired up, ready for the sin.

Sudoku was of course not yet known in the West. It was economics, that halfway house between arts and science, that would occupy me at Cambridge; had it been mathematics, I might have met Sir Michael Atiyah, who lectured there before taking up a chair at Oxford in 1963. It was only when he retired to Edinburgh that I discovered his international fame, and wrote a poem about him, thanks to a comment attributed to his son, "My dad is now too old to solve that problem . . ."

The Algebra of Age

See Anna, Barzillai, Caleb:
that ABC of aged celebrity
turning up in books like Numbers,
remembered by young believers
in the faith of complex sums
like one plus one plus one is one.

See Sir Mike, when 88,
scattering brain cells to the winds of age
but gathering long experience in so much more
than the twist of cubic curves and circumstance:
what corners did he peer around,
what angles opened this home run?

Atiyah (now deceased) was famous for understanding research as 'peering round corners', but I was remarkably uncurious at Cambridge. The great C.S. Lewis was teaching there, but I never attended any of his lectures. Of course, there was a common understanding that lectures were not that important, it was the tutorials that were the cutting edge of learning. It took me years to become more curious about life, and another fifty years before I even visited any of the Cambridge museums.

The Polar Museum, Cambridge

Wrapped in a century of time elapsed,
preserved among a thousand cold displays,
the fiery courage of Shackleton and Scott
soon melts the icecaps of museum ways,
binds exploration, science and humanity.
Now we ruminate: where are today's
wild frontiers? What is left to stretch
us, fetch us forward, lift our gaze
above our phones and narcissistic fun?
Go find some fusion energy from that polar sun!

I resisted the bridge circle who would cheerfully have gambled away my sleep. In those days I was simple and strict in my understanding of the Christian life. I had given up minor betting on horses when I became a Christian, and only succumbed to a form of poker half a century later in a safe domestic setting with our grandchildren. Here is what a real poker player might have written:

The Poker Poem

They got me playing Texas Hold 'em
(that's a fancy brand of poker),
even though I went and told 'em
"Folks, I ain't that kind of joker!"

So at first I gently tholed 'em,
losing most and winning some;
I kept my cool and soon enrolled 'em
in my plan to act real dumb.

It wasn't hard. By then I'd sold 'em
stories of my innocence;
I found I knew just how to mould 'em
into trusting my incompetence.

Gradually I switched, and bowled 'em
googlies, saying "Beginners' luck!";
In the end my cunning rolled 'em
over, making me a good fast buck.

Strange, how folk like us when old em-
bark on a lark like Texas Hold 'em!

At Cambridge I just kept my head down, did some hurdling, and ended up with a decent degree.

But not before I had discovered Iona the previous summer of 1959.

It was George MacLeod, again. He had obviously forgiven, or maybe secretly approved, my smug responses as a Sedbergh schoolboy, and kept me on his radar. Out of the blue he summoned me to the Iona Community Café in Glasgow, and persuaded me that to spend three months as a tourist guide on Iona would be an obvious part of my gap year. Which was why I arrived at the Abbey in May 1960, long before Historic Scotland took over the running of it.

I loved the island. It was indeed 'a thin place', where earth and heaven seem close. I had more opportunity to explore it than most, because of a boat strike which considerably reduced our duties. I relished the attitude of the islanders to impatient visitors, like the American who tried to queue barge in the local shop. The woman at the counter ignored him for as long as she could, and finally looked him firmly in the eye; I overheard her saying, "Young man, the Lord made time and he made plenty of it!"

It was the island of Columba long before it became the island of the Community. Columba was a refugee from trouble in Ireland, alleged to have started over abuse of copyright; he was a leader who became a legend and a saint in Scotland.

Columba

What changed the Irish eagle
to become a Scottish dove?
What gives a man of battles
such a gentle heart of love?

The faithful call it providence,
the sceptics call it spin;
yet people make our history,
and who will call that in?

Academics have argued about history. Did the tree in the forest really fall if no one heard it? Is history what really happened, or just what those who wrote things up claim happened? Over my lifetime the balance of fashion has moved away from the first to the second, but the pendulum will probably swing back to somewhere in the middle.

Providence is a great word, a word which takes the sting out of fate, though there are times to use it and times to keep silent before the mysteries of good and evil, purpose and chance. I have known remarkable answers to prayer, but there are so many times that prayers are not answered as we might wish that I would not expect an atheist to be convinced by that kind of testimony. Archbishop William Temple used simply to say this, when asked: "Answered prayer may be coincidence – but when I pray, coincidences seem to happen!" One way to describe the relation of purpose to chance, which this poem comments on in the context of Genesis chapter 1:

In the Beginning

Seven days to make up everything
from cosmic dust to humankind.
Six days of speaking, one of resting,
days of seeing all was good
in origin, in process and potential.

Seven days to write a poem, sing
a symphony to keep in mind,
hint of word and spirit dancing,
birling stars and swirling galaxies,
making purpose out of chance.

Who knows what other worlds
may sense of their Creator?
We have this book,
we have ourselves,
we have a new beginning.

This, as I said in the Introduction, is a memoir not a biography. Neither however will give the full story. The believer trusts God with the full picture, but with a twist. God is in the business of redemption, which means that parts of our story are going to drop out, and the rest filled out in ways which are (of course) beyond our imagining, though Holy Spirit lets us taste a little of this as healing begins in this life.

We are all so different. I had to pray, "Lord, make me less inhibited" – but I am sure some would be wise to pray the opposite. I am still naturally shy, but I began to develop the confidence to speak in public.

What story we choose to understand ourselves, and others, makes all the difference. And sometimes we need more than one story. Adam was made from the dust of the ground, and so we take our mortality seriously. Humankind were made in the image of God, and so we have also a story of relationship and responsibility, a story which takes us beyond our mortality.

On the west and northern coasts, or on an island, you sometimes find a narrow strip of land between two seas. It has the choice of two tides, each with its claim on the beach running up to that tombolo, as it is called. Each claim is true, with tides to prove it, and only from a higher vantage point can each be given its due place. No doubt this is as true of science and religion, as it is of how we choose to see our stories, with regrets or thankfulness, resignation or hope.

Tombolo

Tide running with a planetful of sorrow,
grief of mine, grief of yours, grief of everyone
passing through the world's hourglass, dragging
like seaweed – or clear, but still heavy, heavy
on us all, prosaic or passionate, crumbling our hope.

Tide running with a long life full of gratitude,
word fashioned, chemistry for soul and body fused
in faith, sea-minerals deposited in scripture and in
testimony; blessed attitude, counter flow decision,
turning on grief, staring down fate, to say 'Thank God!'

What divides these tides which sometimes flow together?
Tombolo, sand spit, land spat in the face of evil, occupied
by one who drowned within the vortex of our grief and
godlessness; then, cast up like Jonah on that beach,
he smiled a holy human smile and said
"Fear not, find out with me the way to surf
those tides of grief and gratitude; my turf
is green with hope and daily bread."

After a while it became clear that George MacLeod and I were occupying different beaches, although I have not lost my admiration for his extraordinary achievement in rebuilding an abbey and founding an alternative to the institution that was the Church of Scotland in those days.

Things came to a head when George decided that it was his duty to make me drink sherry at a party in his house. He recognised, correctly, that I was far too straight-laced. It never occurred to him to suggest to me that the Bible commended alcoholic drink, which was the reason why I later gave up the teetotal way of life inherited from my non-religious father. Instead he tried to command, which did not work, and I never joined the Iona Community.

In other circumstances George MacLeod could be much wiser, as when he needed a local farmer to cut a path through a growing crop up to the local established church; this character, a staunch free churchman, did not like the idea of making it easier to get to the 'auld kirk'; whereupon George with a flash of inspiration asked if the farmer would cut a path *away from* the established church – which he was happy to do.

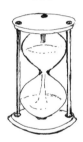

A task which poetry shares with preaching, is to help people see things from a different point of view, to disarm prejudice and turn things right way up. The image of an hourglass comes to mind, an ancient gadget which not only told you when an hour had passed but – like the parables of Jesus – nudged you to consider seeing the world upside down (or right way up).

The Hourglass

We hardly notice how the sand grains pass
our lives, our loves so quickly through the glass;
until that tipping point, we stay cocooned
within a nest of circumstance, attuned
to family noise, the grunts and little farts
that make dull symphony, their counterparts
within the crowd just sounding much the same;
no obvious fuss, no rush to praise or blame
until the shuffle shifts its paradigm
and suddenly we all run out of time,
and fall apart. It's then God flips the scene
to let us see what all things really mean,
and how each tiny grain's a universe
to be explored, for better – not for worse –
and how in every running grain of sand
God travels with us to the promised land.

In those days I was certainly not writing sonnets, let alone distinguishing the Shakespearean style (above) from the Petrarchan. I had written a good number of essays on banking and economic history, and was more concerned with job applications, which happily were a doddle compared to the complexities which companies demand today.

I was also singing songs. I graduated from Scots songs to Schumann's *Dichterliebe*, finding *Ich Grolle Nicht* a great way to sing out the heartbreak of unrequited love (she was the daughter of a stainless steel baron) . . . but how grateful I am now to the Christian discipline which made a virtue of waiting. And as always I sublimated my feelings in hard work.

One of George MacLeod's great ideas was to link work and worship, not only through the liturgy of worship in the abbey but by the use of working men (men, in those days) in the rebuilding programme, and his wider concern to relate faith and work. I wanted to do this in my own life, when I worked in the steel industry after leaving university.

Much later, looking after a Charity which employed an office manager and fundraiser, I wrote a poem for the lady in question. It would have been equally true for myself at this point in life.

Every Job

Every job is a dialogue with many others,
and a fresh journey into myself,
my skills, my strengths, my satisfactions,
my uncertainties and my unknowns.

Every place is a rendezvous
and a path I tread a thousand ways.
Every time is a new opportunity

to grow my neurons and nerve endings,
to discover the mystery of my being,
to catch a smile upon the face of God.

Those were the days when companies rolled out red carpets to attract graduates, but lacking a qualification in metallurgy I could not get a job with Stewarts and Lloyds in Motherwell, and had to settle for United Steel Companies in Sheffield. I chose steel because they were the main customers for the refractory bricks which our family business produced. I was unaware then of the wider world of steel-making in Europe, and its link with the arms industry, which came to my attention much later in France when steel-making was just a memory.

Steel and Schneider

That Schneider family,
forge masters, spell casters,
arms and the men
locked into pursuit
of profit and power.

Le Creusot *their foundry,*
steel town, eyes down
to get their house full
of art and influence,
le château *their bower.*

Bingo! Engineering
dream, that huge steam
hammer, said to crack
a shell and leave
the nut to flower

inside: finesse,
like when the men
designed a theatre
snug inside an old
glass furnace tower.

Schneider, captive to
the charms of arms,
bred understanding
among competitors
that war's their hour.

Old eyes are closed,
staff cut, works shut,
the château *now a shrine*
to lost enchantment
and a game gone sour.

I shared a flat with a Christian friend, and only discovered when he got into trouble with the police that he was homosexual – that was how it was before people 'came out' – but it showed me the depth of mental and spiritual agony involved. We were living in Sheaf Gardens, a street now gone, but it was called after the River Sheaf which still flows under the main station in Sheffield.

There was a lively 'Christian youth scene' and I got involved with the Sheffield Youth Squash, which was led by Peter Fenwick, who later became one of the early leaders of the 'House Church Movement'. He was treasurer of an Anglican Church, and I remember him telling me he was going to move into a new House Church for two years as an experiment, "then I'll go back", he said. I told him he wouldn't, and I was right.

Steel-making was exciting – I settled into a job with Steel, Peech and Tozer in Rotherham, just before the Clean Air Acts began to transform the atmosphere between there and Sheffield; I was doing the operational research necessary as we changed a big open hearth melting shop into what was then the world's biggest electric arc melting shop. In my training I had already learned how to fettle a furnace (firing refractory material horizontally from a shovel to hit the back of the furnace at just the right spot), with the words of a huge Polish first hand melter ringing in my ears: "First time you get it wrong, I show you. Second time, I tell you. Third time, I pick you up and throw you in the furnace!"

I had quickly learned that it was wise to check your ideas by talking with those actually doing the job, and useful night shifts were spent up in the heights with crane drivers. A similar conclusion today might be that we need politicians who have spent time in 'real jobs' . . . as we have an Archbishop of Canterbury who spent time in the oil industry. This poem, written in 2019, harks back to those days. It was inspired by a famous poem by W.S. Graham, *The Nightfishing*, which tells of a fishing trip where the poet finds himself 'one with his companions' as they return from a night's fishing.

Work Study at Steel, Peech and Tozer

"This instant,
bounded by its own grace and all Time's grace,
masters me into its measurement . . ."

W.S. Graham[1]

The hooter blares, the night shift has begun:
melters, mill men scaled to waiting pubs,
the new shift hang their caps and coats on pegs,
check notes and temperatures, begin to swear,

---

1 'The Night Fishing', *New Collected Poems*, Faber, London 2004, 111.

pick up the talk of football, dogs, as if
they'd never been away; their shovels fire
refractory slews to fettle furnace walls,
precision pitch through heat and dust and glare.

To find my place I climb two ladders, swing
myself aboard a crane which crawls the heights,
beside a friendly Pole who knows the ropes,
the cables, hooks and brakes in every detail.
He is not Sheffield born, so we are two
who know we have no local entry rights;
we have no fathers, grandfathers indeed
who bore the hotness, sweated pints of ale.

A clipboard signals my more alien task –
to look, to think, to calculate how many
cranes and ladles, as we change our style
from open hearth to electric arc, the new
cut mixing bowl to tailor make good steel.
We rearrange our minds, for all our poets
die and rise within a second life,
become the argument that sparks the true.

The night wears on, I check my working thoughts
with Jan, we both pontificate on steel
and sensibilities, on death and taxes
probably, the things we share as men
rocked hard within life's complicated cradle,
yet allowed a glimpse of sense we peer
about, above the heavy ladles, dark
with toxic slag, which gives the deadliest burn.

Before the night turns into dawn, the scene
has subtly shifted. Furnaces still teem
their weighty cargos into ladles, molten
steel keeps filling waiting moulds, and fiery
ingots trundle as they did before;
but something in me travels with them, binding
me to melters, mill men, all the human
folk who forge a camaraderie.

But the days of the new electric arc melting shop were numbered. There was a series of takeovers in the steel industry, and in spite of the installation of continuous casting in the 1980s, the works closed in 1993.

At this point I was a small cog in a still large industry, expecting that after a few years I would move back into brick-making, probably in due course to run our own business. We had two factories, one at Castlecary, managed by my cousin Colin Stein, and a newer one at Manuel, between Linlithgow and our old family home at Polmont, managed by my cousin Alastair Stein. Their middle brother Ronald looked after the mines and raw material supply. Another cousin, Kenneth Sanderson, was also involved. The village of Whitecross was built to provide accommodation for men working at Manuel – my father was always proud of providing employment when it was built during the Depression of the 1930s.

He incidentally re-directed Alex Salmond's career, as the former First Minister explained to Kirsty Young on Desert Island Discs in January 2011. Age 15, Alex had decided to leave school, and fancied working at the local Manuel brickworks. He got a holiday job to try it out, thanks to an uncle who was a foreman there. However his mother Mary Salmond had a quiet word with her brother, so that Alex was given unpleasant jobs like shifting anthracite, with the intended result that he decided to go back to school!

I can't remember what started to shake my decision to stay working at Rotherham – although I was offered promotion. It was a niggle at first, which grew until it bore some resemblance to a later poem.

Half Way

This three day halt is nearly half a week,
and I am half way up or half way down
the high Sierra. No half measures, please,
I want to know direction and velocity,
though sitting in this chair I estimate
the speed of movement if the earth stands still
(to make my calculation comfortable)
is zero. That still leaves me flat,
with all my options open: go on up,
or go on down, or rest a while, enjoying
the precision of my careful indecision,
half a lifetime spent with choice collision.

What clinched my decision to give notice happened on a skiing holiday. Eventful because our best man, Peter Ward, broke a leg (it does happen to doctors), and that made it more likely that the Sunday morning would find us at the local Rothiemurchus Church.

The minister was a bit weird (though not this time a wimp), rumoured to have prophetic gifts, and was known to go up the chairlift on a Sunday to take a service on the ski slopes with black robes flapping, a strange bat perched above a snowy gully. He knew me, but not that well. After the service he walked to the churchyard gate beside me. At the gate he turned, looked me in the eye, and said, "Jock, you should be in the ministry, shouldn't you?" I knew immediately he was right.

When I told my mother she looked anxious. It turned out she was fearful that I might be heading for the Church of England instead of the Church of Scotland! I reassured her. The degree of fear, however, from such a staunch Unionist, surprised me – was it suspicion of the English, or only of Anglicans? I can understand why the Episcopal Church of Scotland makes such a meal of their Scottish ancestry – they are definitely 'not Anglicans'!

At that time I was a member of a downtown Anglican Church in Sheffield (and along with a Methodist, on their church council, which was a bit unusual for a Presbyterian, but apparently quite acceptable for a strongly low church Anglican vicar – and bishops have more important things to worry about). Nowadays the Church of Scotland would have looked on me with some suspicion, but in those days before we copied Civil Service procedures I had a ten minute interview at the Church's Head Office. David Steel, parish minister of St Michael's, Linlithgow, vouched for me – and in those informal days, that was all that mattered. Did it help that my uncle Moubray was Lord Lieutenant of the County? Possibly – but David Steel was no respecter of persons; I once overheard him giving our MP Tam Dalyell a row for preparing a speech during the sermon; it was the last time I saw Tam in church, though as he married into a Catholic family there may have been other reasons.

I prepared for transition to theological study by learning New Testament Greek in my lunch hours – a real hour, unlike today's quick bites at the desk. Learning classical Greek at primary school must have been a help.

Not the first of my transitions, as I was to discover later.

Transitions

"Toledo, luz de mi viva" (Marañon)

I come to Toledo
kindled, but not by Rome
like that El Greco.
Nor was Crete my home;
still, I'm aware
of pros and cons, there's
a bed we share
with Stately monsters
(Greek and British).
From an island race,
singular and skittish,
these native artists face
canvas and commissions
cold and raw, make
angular transitions
on the road they take
from unlit youth,
light on somewhere new,
finding their truth
as poets also do.

Chapter Three

EDINBURGH and FINANCE

Having worked in industry, I was now readier for the opportunities of study than when I went up to Cambridge, though I found Edinburgh less demanding academically. But the expectation that lectures should be attended regardless of the skill of the lecturer irked me, and I could not understand why so few lecturers took any trouble to communicate well. Nowadays with the internet as a rival, and TED talks available as a model, I think standards may be higher.

I was fortunate to have great men (as they all were in those days) as my teachers – like Tom and James Torrance, John McIntyre, Alec Cheyne, Andrew Ross and Bill Shaw – they all became friends. Tom Torrance preached at our wedding, and we later hosted his 80th birthday celebration at Carberrry Tower. For two years Bob Walker and I shared a room in the New College residence, with a sloping floor – Bob would one day become famous as the editor of his Uncle Tom Torrance's lectures (which I merely typeset). Bob always says that he woke up to find me reading the Bible in Hebrew, and went to bed while I was reading the Bible in Greek – but he adds that this abruptly stopped when I started serious courting.

I just missed James Stewart, though my wife to be, Margaret Munro, had him for a year as she was a year ahead of me. Later he visited us at Boat of Garten, and I still remember him going down on one knee to say a prayer which looked forward passionately to the coming of Christ. I also heard him give that famous sermon on the Spirit: "Listen to the wind, Nicodemus, listen to the wind!" It went the rounds . . . but then, he also suggested that a good sermon would take 24 hours of work to prepare. Times have changed!

Some of my friends in Scripture Union used to worry when young Christians went off to a theological college, thinking it would destroy their trust in the Bible. This was not an issue at Edinburgh. I had read enough of C.S. Lewis to know that parts of the Bible should not be taken literally, and the experience of college strengthened my respect for the Bible as the word of God as well as the words of men.

There are so many ways of learning. Lectures should be largely for inspiration, not providing facts which are better on a handout or on line. But inspiration is an elusive beast, whether for economics, theology or poetry. In my case the subject was called 'divinity', rather a grand name when you think about it, but all of a piece, I suppose, with the quaint practice of giving ministers the title of 'Reverend'. I was now 25 and a little ahead, potentially, of my earlier thought that I should follow Jesus in not starting ministry till I was thirty.

Musing

How does verse get written?
When the poet is smitten
By great inspiration?
Or deep perspiration
that soaks in like oil
gently easing the soil
in which poetry grows?
Or maybe the wind blows
rich scent of events,
and then nothing prevents
the neurons from firing
out something inspiring.

I suppose that at a deeper level the question of 'inspiration' led me to muse on how we make choices, and how it is that God guides a person – as Christians believe. A continuation of that debate on fate and freedom. I was living with my mother at home in Linlithgow, in the house she got built in the walled garden of Grange, the mansion on the hill where my uncle Moubray Cadell lived. I only remember one sermon from those days, and it wasn't by David Steel – it was by a visiting preacher from Wellington Church in Glasgow; it had three points: predestination, freewill, and the grace of God; I put in the second 'Oxford comma' to emphasise how my understanding of God was beginning to integrate the other two ideas.

Fate and Freedom

The Book of Ecclesiastes

So you've tried it on already?
The shoe fits, for a while, if you can afford it,
but don't collect shoes, or women, or wealth:
for a collectible, try wisdom.

And keep your mouth shut.
Look, and learn – though knowledge hurts.
Pain and pleasure come and go, but proverbs
make you smile awhile.

Enjoy being young, and alive.
That's the time to know the God who made you.
Don't lose your head in books or beer,
and hedge your bets a bit.

Are things just getting worse?
You must be getting old and crabbit. OK,
but wisdom beats nostalgia every time.
Ask more intelligent questions.

Let God into your mind.
God can handle bad stuff better than you;
God doesn't need the devil for an excuse;
God will sort things out one day.

It may well be written:
"A time for this, a time for that."
Think written up, not written down
as by a moving finger.

Animals and humans die.
We share our genes with mice and monkeys,
conscious of our limits. God, give us
please, more light on living.

We hang up mental pictures
and they go and surf our brain waves.
Rob Pinsky's dire one or desired one[1]
is left an open question.

David Steel was sometimes controversial. He had a tendency (I was later told by his successor) to come to Session meetings with the minute already written in his head. One of his ploys was to replace the stone crown on the top of the tower of St Michael's – removed some time before because of its weight – with an aluminium crown. Although it lost its colour much more quickly than promised, the crown was a dramatic assertion that the arts and religion should support one another: and as I remember Dr Steel himself saying at the time, it was like throwing your hat in the air to the glory of God.

1 From his poem *Ode to Meaning*.

That featured in a later poem, along with the storm which blew the boats we were looking after for Scripture Union right out of Linlithgow Loch and beached near Bonnytoun House, which my grandmother once occupied at the east end of Linlithgow Loch:

A Train of Memories

Today the train traversed my childhood,
pointed out the Ochils, where
my bare feet pounded the summer grass,
and Castle Campbell gloomed over the glen;
slowed down outside Linlithgow,
where the new crown squats slender
above St Michael's Church.

The train picked up my younger years,
sat them down beside me, chattering
about tormentil, trefoil, thistles
when my eyesight missed a beat;
opened the files on that storm
which lifted all the boats by the Peel,
parked them high and dry at Bonnytoun.

The train stopped only for a minute,
drew the curtains once again
upon those early Hillfoots years
so full of passion, power and promise,
scattered somewhere, lost
within the hard disk of our times.
I am left, searching for the rhymes.

I grew up in the days when university education was still a minority pursuit, and except for a few at the sharp end, seemed much less competitive. Certainly I spent a large amount of time on other activities, including a visit to the Notting Hill Housing Trust one summer, with a group of students painting flats. Other activities included becoming chair of the Divinity Students Council at Edinburgh, following Peter Millar (later Warden at Iona) in that role. That year it was the turn of New College to convene the meeting of the Councils of the four Scottish divinity colleges, which gave me the chance to meet others who would turn out to be future church leaders. One of these was David Ogston, who as minister of St John's Church in Perth was to become famous for using the Scots leid in worship.

Previously I had been the Council treasurer, and before that treasurer of the Cambridge University Pipe Band; my most distinguished activity was once leading the band the wrong way down a one way street in Cambridge, to the chagrin of the police. But I still find myself more than fifty years later treasurer of three active Charities – the habits of not saying 'no' die hard.

At the time I had to be my own treasurer, because some family trusts were vesting and landing me with a large amount of capital. I had already formed the habit of giving away 10% of my income, but this was something else. Over the years it allowed me to set up a number of trusts for different purposes, and it gave me a confidence in dealing with money – lack of confidence, I think, is the main reason why it is often hard to find a treasurer for community and charitable enterprise. I remember writing to my stockbroker Mark Sherriff, who was also session clerk of a church near Doune, and warning him that I intended to give away the capital I had; wisely he didn't reply; in fact it has taken me a lifetime to do that.

Giving away a proportion of income is something that Christians generally do, though it need not be 10% – I often say that some should give more, and many less than that. Giving should be a joy, not a burden. Where did the money go? In my case, half to my local church, and half into a separate bank account to use wherever it seemed right.

Giving is one of the things that make us human; one of the many bad things about poverty is that it may turn folk into receivers rather than givers (though the poor are in proportion to their income usually far more generous than the wealthy) – whereas we should all be both to some extent. An argument perhaps for the concept of 'basic income' which as I write is being trialled in Scotland and Finland.

Land Value Taxation is another change which most economists would support – as did politicians like Lloyd George and Winston Churchill in the past. However, with any radical change of income or taxation there will be winners and losers, and short of a revolution a country needs to be in a healthy financial state so it can cushion the blow to the losers.

'Treasurer' is one of those words that can be applied to anything from a local sports club to a nation, as with Scotland which once had a 'Lord High Treasurer'. This poem, published recently in the anthology *Umbrellas of Edinburgh*, features the gentleman on top of the pillar in St Andrew Square, who occupied something of that role after the Union of 1707. It was written when the south side of the Square was a mess of reconstruction.

On the Square

Tangled rod ends dangle in their metal webs,
no longer able to conceal their reinforcement
of the hard core guts of money making
in this once rich square. High cranes take days
to launder work space, disengage blue cladding,
grab at rubbish concrete with their jagged jaws,
worrying it like a dog, dropping it in clouds
of dust controlled by well-aimed water sprays.

Such rough treatment of two million hours
of history . . . on his column, Viscount Melville
notices and gives an angry cough: first trams,
and now a shopping mall, what next, a helipad?
Is this the distant fruit of that enlightened brilliance
which propelled us to pan-European heights?
Or is it more the slow unpicking of Establishment,
so should we click at once on 'like', or be heart-sad?

The Square began with Dundas House, which soon became
the Royal Bank head office, with its hall and features
starring in some banknotes still in circulation.
The British Linen Bank was built upon its flanks
in 1806, and taken over by the Bank of Scotland.
The Union bank (now RBS) then gobbled up
the National Bank; with a sense of dèja vu we ask,
'They regulate their clients . . . who regulates the banks?'

The famous lived there in the Square – Lord Henry
Brougham and David Hume, who hosted intellectual
dinner parties, probably without miraculous content.
He could not see arrive at number five a later
theist neighbour, National Bible Society, spreading
scriptures as the great philosopher once exported
his ideas. Today, instead of books and sparkling wine
and conversation, yawns a flat and empty crater.

Scottish Provident sold their Life Assurance first
in 1837. Their actuaries ruled like kings, and
one chipped daily golf balls from his office window
perfectly onto the grassy centre, till his status
changed from mild celebrity to minor criminal.
Spot on the Millennium, Abbey bought them over,
asset stripped them, took the loot to Glasgow
dodging history's question: 'Just how will they rate us?'

And where is old St Andrew in this pilgrimage of fame?
How does he match young Vincent Street and Charlotte Square,
with his chosen site gazumped by Melville's mansion?
Seems like money talks, and sainthood walks a furlong
further west to build a modest church in George Street.
On the demolition site, some railings shape a cross
held up on listed buildings pleading for survival,
while the Planners hold the key to right and wrong.

Dundas was 'on the square': at least he got the name
'Grand Manager of Scotland', or 'Ninth King Harry'.
Now labels cover all: this is a project shared
with Peveril Securities, though under Standard Life,
to turn the corridors of high finance into the lanes
between deodorant and toothpaste, with a nod
to history above – some office space, and at the top
the penthouse flats. Here is no sub-standard life.

For a short time one of our newspapers published a cartoon featuring the sassy male Vincent Street and the snooty female Charlotte Square, obviously meant to take off Glasgow and Edinburgh. Sadly it ceased, perhaps it was too near the bone. Edinburgh certainly takes itself seriously, proud of its philosophers. Two of its most famous are found sculpted near the top of the High St. David Hume we will return to. Adam Smith is the other.

Adam Smith

He thought well. He meant well. He lived well.
He deserves this statue by the City Chambers
to the author of The Wealth of Nations.

Is he not the father of free enterprise?
He has earned this jacket with eleven buttons,
this cloak, this curled wig, this reputation.

Now his eyes and lips are bronze, to match
the hearts of those who cherry-pick his writings,
leaving out his checks and balances to power.

It's a shame that Adam Smith is renowned only as an economist, and hailed as the father of capitalism. He was a moral philosopher who would be profoundly shocked by many of the things done in the name of free enterprise today. Actually, John Calvin is sometimes hailed as the father of capitalism, because he distinguished between loans for production and loans for consumption, and allowed interest to be charged on the former. Like Smith he would of course be appalled at the level of personal debt today.

When Lehman Brothers filed for bankruptcy on Sept 15th 2008, economics was shown not to be the exact science that Gordon Brown assumed when he claimed that 'boom and bust' were history. This mirage of precision appeared because of the recent emphasis on economic modelling; but models are only as good as the assumptions they make.

In 2011 Tomas Sedlacek, adviser to Vaclav Havel, wrote a bestseller called *The Economics of Good and Evil*, which inspired this poem.

Macro-economic Forecasting

Ask Xenophon, the first economist,
when to plant your crops: he will say,
"I know my limitations".
Ask Xenophon, citizen of Athens,
when to go to war: he will tell you,
"Go to Delphi, ask
the Oracle to predict State revenue."
Poets were the ones who spelt the truth
of cereals and credit.

Ask Pharaoh how to run a surplus:
he will say, "I dreamt of cows and corn,
and with a little help
from my first minister, ex Hebrew slave,
I set our tax at twenty full per cent
for seven golden years.
Prophets make quite good economists
in lean times too, I came to think
– austerity made me rich."

Ask the Matrix Oracle for advice:
it's still that delphic "Neo, know thyself".
As Government Adviser,
you might profit by her wisdom,
leave politicos to call elections,
hazard boom or bust.
Pollsters love the chance to forecast
people's choices. Poets write their words
as if they matter.

In those days I was learning to write sermons, not poetry, and not yet concerned with politics – it was Africa which awoke that interest, but before that I had three years living in Crieff, where I had a job organising summer missions – meaning that I would spend a lot of the summer taking piles of mattresses round Scotland in a minibus, to be dumped in church halls for teams of up to 60 people, then uplifted after the mission period was over.

In those days it was taken for granted that Scotland was a Christian country where kids should be entertained and inspired by the Christian story on beaches, camp sites and in public parks – such a far cry from our present culture where atheism is now respectable, and Christianity suspect.

What lies at the root of this change? Culturally, the experience of the 1960s and their freedoms were a key, but intellectually Freud and Marx had a place, and especially Darwin – such an irony, when you think how many Christian leaders were happy to embrace his ideas. Darwin was a complex character, not least because he was married to a strong believer; he struggled with the question of faith, but certainly did not dismiss it glibly as some do today.

Darwin did not jump into biological research. Early on he considered becoming a priest, changed his mind and tried studying medicine at Edinburgh, but left that after a year.

Charles Darwin

Dropping out of medicine is dramatic,
heading out to distant seas is more so.
Loss to Edinburgh, but gain to science:
'Darwin, under the guise of a foe,
doing the work of a friend.'

Here is the man who never lost all faith,
though tragically bereaved of daughter Ann.
Unnatural selection, you might think,
sour challenge to any eternal plan,
or easy make and mend.

He chose to be a scientist, not a priest;
God does not compete with science for space
and loves to do things gradually, let
raw predation bless the human race
and make good in the end.

David Hume and Charles Darwin, often seen as enemies of religion, were indeed 'friends'. In different fields, and in quite different ways, they disposed of bad arguments for God.

"Why did Darwin drop out?" I was once asked.

"Well, he enjoyed helping Robert Grant to label sponges and things like that in his spare time, but the medicine part left him squeamish. However, I think what really scared Darwin away from Edinburgh after just one year was meeting the young radicals, who liked what Darwin was already saying about biology, and saw it as grist to their anti-establishment mill."

"Young radicals? The people who would walk and talk on 'Radical Road' near the Salisbury Crags?"

"Yes. Darwin was well-connected with English men of property and influence, and didn't want his ideas to be used to upset the order of society. He started at Edinburgh University in 1825, just a quarter of a century after the French Revolution.[2] In fact he only published the first edition of *The Origin of Species* in 1859; some say the delay was because Darwin did not want to upset his wife who held more traditional views, but I think there were others he feared upsetting."

---

2   Edmund Burke and others used to warn against the social instability which they believed would follow from the atheistic ideas of the French Revolution. The empirical sciences should stay close to natural theology and "keep the working classes from fomenting rebellion". (Peter Harrison's Gifford Lectures of 2011, chapter 6)

Nowadays the only people likely to be upset by Darwin are those who take a very literal view of Genesis and dislike the idea of evolution as a biological theory.

Creation Controversies

Did God fine-tune that blind, rough hewn
Darwinian contraband?
We call the peacock's feathers beautiful,
the naked mole-rat's habits ugly
(cue that rap on fecal pap
that no one ever makes).

A second guess for all the mess
that evolution hazards?
We're glad that human brains grew big,
but draw the line at dystrophies
(the dismal scenes from human genes
gone just a bit astray).

When God said 'great', not 'second-rate'
to natural selection,
let's say somewhere between day four
and six in Genesis, perhaps
he had in mind a future, kind
and chosen with his Son.

"Richard Dawkins thought of Darwin as 'the devil's chaplain', didn't he?" said another friend more recently.

"Dawkins used that phrase, which Darwin himself used, as the title of one of his books. He certainly saw Darwin on the side of the scientific devils, who were of course angels of light as far as Dawkins was concerned."

"Darwin must have been a thorn in the side of theologians."

"Not really. The quotation in verse one [of the poem on Darwin, opposite] comes from the English churchman Charles Kingsley, and the well-known Scottish Christian leader Henry Drummond was a keen Darwinist. Darwin helped people to see that unless God is everywhere, he is nowhere. The current jargon for that is 'panentheism' but the older word is 'immanence.'"

It is with the rise of Creationism in America in the 20th century that Darwin became such a bogeyman – but in my years at Crieff I don't recall this as an issue at all. My interest in biology was totally focused on a young woman I had met at New College, Margaret Munro, a divinity student who had come with a diploma from Edinburgh College of Art. She still won't let me publish my more explicit love poems, but here is a modest one.

Anniversary

Those perfectly riveting veins
surmount the beaded catenary
of a necklace gifted
that hopeful year before the Referendum.
Beneath, your dress a bare parabola
above the blue flowers,
beautiful and beckoning,
as we sit engaged
by this ageing artery of life
which still pulses between us.

Back at college, Margaret and I had been on a summer mission team together, so we had seen how we each functioned under pressure. Nearer Christmas, I asked her for a date twice – each time she had something else on. I was trying to work out what that meant, but I decided to try once more, and she agreed. We went to the university carol service, sat down, and while we were chatting realised someone had sat down beside us: on looking round we found it was Margaret's brother! Happily Alick went back to his student flat afterwards, so we walked across the Meadows, I proposed and she said yes.

Soon after that I was invited up to Turriff to meet her parents, and follow the old custom of asking her father's permission; we were of course equally nervous, but all went well, and I was able to share with his brother Willie in leading a family gathering in song, in my case from the piano. It was a busy time. I had just agreed to go and work with Bill Shannon for a probationary year, and two days before the journey north I had to take 'that funeral' at the request of my headmaster's family – a baptism of fire.

Margaret's parents were remarkable people. In a family of farmers, her father James Munro was the youngster who had to find another way of life, and became a prize-winning architect who settled for a country practice. Her mother was at various times a theatre nurse, a social worker and a dietician. They were married in 1939 and separated for much of the war.

There was a difficult period just after the war when her mother Peggy suffered from what she later described as being like bubonic plague. Margaret had measles and mumps and was living with an aunt, Peggy was in the Turriff Cottage Hospital. One day her husband James came in to visit, and was greeted by the nurse, "Oh Mr Munro, I'm sorry . . ." He got to the bedside to find the doctor writing out the death certificate.

At that moment Peggy opened her eyes, and started to make her recovery. Later she described her experience. "I remember going through a tunnel towards a bright light. It was warm and balmy. Then I heard a voice saying, 'Peggy, go back, you have work to do." She did, and brought up her two children Margaret and Alick (who became a doctor and worked in London).

Margaret by this time had finished her degree at New College, with her four years at art college counted as the first year of an ordinary BD. She financed this by selling paintings, and with help from Bill Shaw, then a member of staff with a great way of finding bits and bobs of bursaries for folk who needed them. Among all her other attributes, she lived by her Turriff Academy school motto, 'as wise as serpents and as harmless as doves'.

We were married in Palmerston Place Church on 20th September 1969, the year Neil Armstrong and Buzz Aldrin set foot on the moon. Space exploration had very different connotations for me at the time, though I think the three of us would have agreed that the moon had a definite aura of romance. Barcelona has a restaurant called *El Beso y la Lluna* – in a free translation of the Catalan, *A Kiss in the Moonlight*.

Moonlight Kiss

He wheels away his cello on a trolley.
We are not the most paying of guests,
seated on the plaça with paella and moussaka.

In any case, he does not claim monopoly
in the arts of entertainment. His interests
served, he leaves El Beso y la Lluna

to Jordi playing saxophone, whose volley
of notes might prove an earner. Such contexts
weave our words and sketch books into one, spark a

sudden memory of Joan Miró, and the folly
of dividing poetry and painting, which suggests
the moon might see a kiss approaching sooner.

Joan Miró (Juan in Spanish) was a famous artist, who believed that poetry and painting belonged together, music naturally to the ears of this couple, although we both stick firmly to our respective lasts. In this next poem, written in the gardens pictured opposite, I had to give Margaret a Spanish name; the title reads like bad French, but in fact is Catalan.

Jardins de la Tamarita

In Catalonia they seek pleasure and play
on the dusty floor of a botanic garden.

This is where the boys of Barcelona
measure lusty kickabouts against their dreams
of a professional future. As they say,
Barça is more than a football club.

Kike fingers his bansuri, watches his son
run on the hard ground. His melody repeats.
This scene is found, playing, all over Europe.

Margarida sits, finishes an ink sketch
of that gnarled clifftop eucalyptus, which
might be talking to the sky about the life
of every person walking, running down below.

In Catalonia they catch leisure, and lay
it down to flower in the human jungle.

Our theological teacher Tom Torrance was kind enough to preach at our wedding service in Palmerston Place Church and we escaped on our honeymoon with only the loss of my shoes to enthusiastic friends. Our first night was in the Shap Wells Hotel, and we continued to Athens, where we borrowed a car from the brother-in-law of a friend, only discovering later that it was uninsured. That friend was George Dragas, who moved from the Greek Evangelical Church to become a well-known Greek Orthodox theologian.

George was also an artist. When I was fitting out a bunkhouse at Millfield, our Boat of Garten property, I put wood strippings on the walls and flat boards on the ceiling. George thought them rather plain, so painted a variety of insects upon them; I don't think many occupants of a top bunk enjoyed gazing up at creepy-crawlies.

On the island of Cos, we hired a tandem. It gave Margaret a terrible vision of married life, being at the back and unable to steer,

and it took a few years to sort that out. But there was an unexpected 'prophecy' which gave her hope; when we signed into the hotel, not of course in clerical costume, we were greeted by the comment, "So, you are priests?" – this was said in the plural, in that traditional Orthodox setting where women are excluded from that calling.

We began our married life in Crieff, living in a house with a minute kitchen area, which did not stop Margaret baking, as so many did in those days of clearly defined roles. She has always been good at multi-tasking, so also managed to fit in a Probationary Year at the North Church in Perth; getting to a Sunday morning service on time changed her from a cautious to a speedy driver, even when pregant with our first child, Dorothy, born on a Christmas Day in Perth Royal Infirmary.

Margaret has always managed to bake a rich Christmas cake, thanks to a lady I met during one of my attachments to an Edinburgh congregation:

Mrs Binnie's Cake

She is making the cake,
Mrs Binnie's Christmas cake.
I have to interrupt my study
to digest this ritual, make
more than mention of a woman,
a good plain Edinburgh woman,
a Liberton Northfield woman
who knew when and how to bake.

She is making the cake,
our wedding cake it was to be,
but she – I speak of Mrs Binnie –
fell off a chair and broke
two ribs, so one year late
I drove the lady up to Crieff
to share her secret recipe
with Margaret and me.

She is making the cake,
Mrs Binnie's special cake;
beside her is a faded postcard,
dated that first year of marriage,
and our Golden Wedding now
just nine months off; no wonder
it is half a pound of raisins,
ounces for the cherries and mixed peel,
and the temperature in Fahrenheit.

She is making the cake,
Mrs Binnie's blessed cake,
remembering her pilgrimage,
because this cake can come to birth
in any kitchen, with the proper coupling,
word and woman. Mrs Binnie had to use
every single bowl within the house,
wrap the tin with newsprint, when
the Soviets downed the U2 spy plane,
and Bono born in May that year.

She is making the cake,
Mrs Binnie's Christmas cake,
mixing yokes and fruit by hand
as mothers, grannies used to do.
I remember how a woman
blended heaven and earth, brought
a miracle to birth, and sang
her golden recipe, 'in the name of love'
for us, and such as us, to raise us up,
the Mrs Binnies of this world.

My boss, Bill Shannon, was warden of St Ninian's Centre, which was gutted and rebuilt during my time there. By dint of helping Stanley Heavenor, minister of St Michael's Church, with his youth fellowship I was allowed to count these three years as my required probationary period to qualify as a minister of the Church of Scotland. Sunday mornings were normally spent doing pulpit supply in neighbouring vacant churches; for this we recruited a number of divinity students, and this provided a significant part of the Centre's income.

The Centre had been founded by the evangelist D.P. Thomson, a legendary martinet who by this time had retired and mellowed dramatically in his old age. He and George MacLeod used to spar on the floor of the General Assembly; both military figures, although DP (as he was known) had been invalided out of First War service; George MacLeod did not become a pacifist till later in his life.

Agnostic Memorial

Sombre heroes . . .
A century of mist
swirls between us;
now you see them,
now you don't.

Conscientious fighters
or objectors feathered
and detested, spat on.
Callow officers, and
underclassed young men.

Trenches, mud, gas,
loyalty and courage,
folly and betrayal.
A good war for some,
rotten for most.

Do we really
remember them?
Does the universe
notice our passing?

We ran a Saturday Ski Club, driving people up to Glenshee and offering overnight accommodation at St Ninian's. For this I had to pass (at the second attempt) an exam to be a Ski Party Leader. I like to think that we were more skilled using the long skis of the time than people who use the much shorter skis fashionable today. We had our adventures . . . just before publication I remembered a frightening experience when we had been doing some modest ski touring; it was in a poetry group in Stagg's Bar, Musselburgh, and we had been asked to write a poem about spiders:

Whiteout

I never thought a spider lost till
it was there, static, stuck
on the floor of the bath,
and I was in that whiteout
on Carn Aosda in Glenshee,
with no way out of the universe.

It was time to find a way on from Crieff. For a short while I thought of further study with David Cairns at Aberdeen University, but in the end we asked the Overseas Council (as it was called) of the Church if they could use a missionary of my character. In those days husbands were accompanied by wives, nowadays it would be a joint appointment.

They suggested that I go to Chilema Lay Training Centre in Malawi, but suddenly that changed to Kenya. Years later I discovered that the Malawi missionaries had objected to having someone labelled as in the evangelical tradition thrust upon them – an irony considering that I was later to follow the Iona Community member Colin Day as warden of Carberry Tower.

I borrowed a Kikuyu grammar and started language study.

Chapter Four

KENYA

Although Kenya was independent, the Church of Scotland was still regarded as the mother church of the Presbyterian Church of East Africa, and indeed a key part of the independence movements of several African countries. Scots and English were heavily invested in the colonial history of Africa, although they left a legacy of separate Anglican and Presbyterian churches.

Quaint as it seems today, the late Kenneth Kaunda, whose father David Kaunda was a mission evangelist, made a special pilgrimage to our Church Headquarters at 121 George St to thank us for what we had done to help achieve the independence of Zambia. Later I would use the theme of one of Kaunda's books to reflect on what we did or did not pass on to our children.

Letter to my Children

I am borrowing this title
to make my own confession:
often guilty of neglect,
putting projects before people,
power stuck like treacle on the fingers.

I know how vision can be used
to justify the busy hours
which growing children miss
but never leave behind.

I am borrowing this title
from someone not in fashion:
Humanist and Christian,
mostly absent father,
preacher and presider,
founder of a nation scarred

by dreams which plunged to earth
like falling comets (in his words).

He made unlikely pilgrimage
to thank our Scottish church
which helped to birth his Zambia.
Now, I make his book a shrine.

I am borrowing this title
because I share his passion:
education broad as paradise,
values moored in good religion
not left drifting with the vote
or aped from this or that celebrity.

Human is, or not, in every land . . .
I hope my children understand.

My main task was to produce a booklet on some relevant subject like 'salvation' or 'stewardship' or 'politics' each year in Kikuyu (sometimes also in Swahili and English), then sell and teach it all round the country. For this I had a senior African colleague; he was the brother of the Mayor of Nairobi, and the only time I felt I risked deportation was when I tried in public to tell a joke about him which would have been funny in English but turned out not at all funny in Kikuyu. I have never been good at telling jokes.

I had a lot to learn, as well as two languages. Swahili is easy – a second language for everyone except a few tribes at the coast, and pronounced like Italian – it took me six weeks to preach (badly) in Swahili. Kikuyu is difficult, a tonal language, and it was six months before I could preach (badly) in Kikuyu.

Margaret did some painting in Kenya, but always complained that it was hard to paint when twenty curious local children were crowding round. In Scotland it was midges and tourists, but fifty years later it is different; with the advent of social media and new ideas of what is 'correct', people are no longer curious.

During our three and a bit years in Kenya I thought seriously about politics for the first time, as I noticed what a difference it made in the lives of ordinary people. We set up a small factory to give employment, and sold potato crisps to East African Airways until some of our staff thought they could get more packets into a box if they pierced the packets to let the air out.

Whatever I managed to do or not do for the people of Kenya, living in Africa did far more for me. I discovered freedom in worship, seeing how women would feed babies during a church service, how people could dance a liturgy, and how a tiring preacher could be rescued by a song from the congregation. The church was still enlivened by the earlier East African Revival, and people would walk as much as 50 miles to come to the teaching.

The singing could be inspiring, provided people stopped trying to sing hymns in a pentatonic imitation of a Scottish tune, and really went local (as other tribes seemed to have done more readily – the Kikuyu were still doggedly trying to stay Scottish, at least when we arrived). But there were songs of the Revival, as I was reminded just last year, when one turned up at a conference held in the Octagon at Lee Abbey in Devon.

Mungu ni Mwema

The song slept for fifty years,
bedded lovingly in his memory.
It woke, no time to yawn
before it danced around the Octagon
and laughed at all those miles
travelled between dusk and dawn.

I learned a great deal from African colleagues, some of whom became good friends – like Samuel Ngure, the local minister, and John Mburu, who later took over the literature work I was doing.

So much was extraordinary, even the first house we lived in, which had a strange journey in pieces from Britain; after we moved to another house it was occupied by the Kaplinsky family, whose daughter Natasha played with our daughter Dorothy; later Natasha would become a TV news presenter. But Margaret suffered, left alone for long periods, her lungs already weakened by the privations of her own student years.

Kenya Days

Thogoto

The house travelled by boat, a Victorian flat pack
of engineering and assumptions. (We went by air.)
It reached the Red Sea, sank, and then, with
all its mental baggage and imperial stubbornness,
was resurrected, to be home for Whites in Kenya.

Salted survivor, stilted verandah, it waited to embrace
two modern missionaries in spidery darkness.
At night a herd of elephants trumpeted in threat
while Margaret cowered with our baby daughter –
till we discovered that the hyrax, rabbit look-a-like
possessed nocturnal powers of voice projection.
We escaped from 'the Banguru' (Bungalow);
instead of locals calling it 'kwa Stein', it welcomed
other Europeans, and transformed itself to
'Kwa Kaplinsky', nurturing Natasha to cast news
one day on Channel Five, UK. What news
would I cast here in Kenya? What complex character,
what unknown places lay beneath our gospel keenness?

Margaret breathed the dusty roads, and suffered,
homesick while her husband worked all over Kenya;
memories of dust, and my own dullness to her feelings,
disguised by language, liturgy and literature: flowing
streams of foamy type, so much in demand, well-checked,
spell-checked English, Swahili and Kikuyu text.
Dreaming of my dictionary to punt Kikuyu idiom
I worked, blind to what was happening to her lungs.

Naivasha

On holiday together, Margaret came alive with art.
Islands full of birds, those paintings take me back
to lovely Lake Naivasha, reds and blues and greens
still crossed in tree shapes on her canvas.
Meeting of Maasai and Kikuyu, and the bus I guided
through the bush to build a school one single day,
and feast on fresh killed cow by night.

Chogoria

They walked for fifty miles to knock about
my pale white lack of hunger for the news
of how real faith could change the life of now,
and why the Kenyan church no longer needed us.
Privilege of teaching, privilege of listening
to their stories, privilege of breaking dawn
in Meru country; and far more, awaking
worship freedom in my life. Let me describe
a service where the congregation move, and
dance a liturgy of love and prayer and hope,
without a word, except the glorious presence
of the Word beyond all words: a touch of heaven.
Or if the preacher talks, and talks too long,
the people throw him songs, and wander out
to pee or have a chat. Inside the women suckle,
and rejoice in gospel improvised on Kenyan soil.

Budapest

János was a colleague there, who taught theology.
His widow Judit asked me to translate one chapter
for a friend whose life was near its end – a gift
to him, while time remained for gifts like these.
I did so gladly, re-immersed in Kenyan days, and
Mau-Mau, courage and a crooked history.
And my special Kenyan friends? Ngure killed himself,
while Mburu nearly died in traffic. What remains
is only this: "to live is Christ, to die is gain".

The reference near the end is to János Pásztor, a Hungarian colleague whose wife wrote a book on her experiences in Kenya during the difficult Mau Mau time, and asked me to translate one particular chapter quickly from Hungarian to English for David Philpott, who was seriously ill. David was a former colleague at Limuru Theological College, and later made a huge contribution to Kenya and the wider Church through his service as Scholarship Secretary for the World Council of Churches.

Our local youth fellowship once travelled into Maasai country in a bus with corrugated iron sheets on the roof, so we could literally build a school in a single day (and then celebrate, feasting on a cow which was killed for the occasion). Actually it included a severe test of my faith. I had gone, once, in a car, through the bush to the building site, a number of miles east of Lake Naivasha. So when the day came, I was told, "You can guide the bus driver" as it appeared no one else on the bus had actually been there! With my memory for topography as poor as my memory for names, I did a lot of praying on that journey. It was much easier writing up the story for *Life and Work* afterwards.

After we left 'the Bungalow' we had a smaller house with a big garden of vegetables, maize, and small bananas known as *tūthūngū* ('little Europeans' – a European is *mūthūngū*). We inherited an elderly African gardener, Njoroge, whose abilities included digging a new *kīoro* (latrine pit) over 20ft deep but not much more than 2ft x 2ft wide. Mind you, that pales in comparison with the 90 ft well that the naturalist John Muir dug himself through sandstone, on his father's farm in Wisconsin – it took him months and he nearly died of carbonic acid gas poisoning!

Njoroge

His face had seen us all:
his patient ears accepted graciously
our first Kikuyu words
for 'yes' and 'no' and 'how are you today?'
His ancient, nodding head
appeared above a bicycle at 7am
each day, come rain, come shine,
and moved in front of him to
park himself, and bike, behind
the termite-chewed verandah.

What filled his weathered days?
His work of course, his memories, and maize.

That poem came out of a workshop when we were invited to write a poem on 'the weathered days of everyone'. In fact, weather from July to September, the cold season, was quite Scottish at 6,000ft above sea level. Not a bad height and climate for growing coffee, in fact.

Barista Dreams

> *Coffee soars:*
> *transcending cup or mug*
> *it feels its steamy way into the soul*
> *to settle scores,*
> *to open pores of understanding,*
> *lubricate negotiation of a deal,*
> *and knock on doors*
> *unvisited and maybe unimagined*
> *by the guy without a bean.*
>
> *Coffee rhymes:*
> *not in a mundane sense*
> *like 'coffee rhymes with toffee';*
> *no, coffee chimes*
> *with Sufi rhythm, gently whirling*
> *till the body wakes and stretches*
> *into leisure times*
> *unknown, so unafforded*
> *by the guy without a bean.*
>
> *Coffee shocks:*
> *English kings and Prussian emperors,*
> *Ottomans, all tried to ban it*
> *from their docks*
> *as heresy, subversive, or not kosher*
> *for the Jews and Turks and Mormons,*
> *as it rocks*
> *the mental coffers, safely populated*
> *by the guy without a bean.*
>
> *Coffee earns:*
> *It's worth a bob or two to those*
> *who import, roast and package it.*
> *Whoever learns*
> *the story of its harvesting, could buy*
> *Fair Trade, support the farmer,*
> *so he overturns*
> *the exploitation of the crop now sweated*
> *from the guy without a bean.*

Coffee hooks:
so Starbucks, Brew Lab, Steampunk
thrive on pressured percolation;
jargon spooks
us with decoction, drip filtration
and much studied preparation.
But the books
about addiction hold no interest
for the guy without a bean.

Coffee spoils:
if you boil it, waste it, spill it.
But it neatly foils loneliness;
a drink soon oils
the rust of solitude, inspires
that kind but risky invitation,
and uncoils
the wardrobe of a hedgehog heart,
to wrap a coat of friendship
round the guy without a bean.

Coffee is grown on the slopes of Mt Kenya, known locally as *kīrī nyaga,* God's resting place. For the Kikuyu traditionally, there was a high God, but *Ngai ndīgiagiagwo,* God is not to be pestered – an attitude to life I found identical to that held by many fellow-workers at home. I recall a conversation with a bricklayer in Manuel Brickworks (where I used to work in school holidays), who told me it was important to believe in God but not bother him much – "that keeps things sweet," he said.

For the same reason, Kikuyus did not normally climb the top two peaks of Mt Kenya, although there is a legend that one day two European climbers struggled to the top of Batian, only to find an African sitting there with bare feet. He must have known English, because when they asked "What on earth are you doing up here?" he is said to have replied, "I come up every year to commune with God!"

Things were certainly different on top of Mt Sinai, which Margaret and I climbed, mainly on camels, at the time of our 25th wedding anniversary. There the Bedouin had a café doing a roaring trade with the hundreds of Nigerians who used to come up there on pilgrimage every year. [see top of next page]

Mt Kenya, even the lower peak of Lenana which I climbed, managing to avoid pulmonary oedema, was seriously cold. When we went on holiday to the coast at Mombasa, it was another story. And the shells were beautiful . . . this one had a hole in it.

Space on the Beach

A hollow shell
jauntily curled into a beret
on a balding brow of white and brown;
a holed spacecraft,
vulnerable to atmosphere,
a landed, sanded piece of ocean debris.

My fingers touch
and feel their way across
the contours, gently mountaineering
over ribs
which cut genetic space
across the spiral. Hold it, turn it over,

see that empty
silver spiral tuck itself away
and make a horn to funnel sea-sound
round and round,
filling my willing ears
like fingers pressing, beckoning me

to listen,
journey to the stars,
swim into orbit on a sea of colour
bold, unfolded
from this fragile conch
like Venus riding into space.

My love of language, and languages, must have come alive in Kenya. I was dismayed to find that some young people knew English but not their own mother tongue – just as many Highland Scots grew up speaking English but not Gaelic. The history of the British Isles is complex, and will not be simply resolved, even by Scottish independence (which we voted for in the Referendum of September 2014).

I was equally dismayed to find hardly any youngsters knew their own proverbs – so I started collecting Kikuyu sayings, with the help of one or two small booklets still available. I even planned, had I returned after furlough, to publish a Kikuyu colloquial dictionary – looking back, an absurd if noble ambition for someone only three years in the country. I had not yet learned my limits, or even to learn from the birds.

Writing is for the Birds

The magpie nods and struts
and pecks at the geranium,
disappears a while, and then is seen
in studied, focused idleness.
Compulsive thief, he steps across
the limits others feel.

The pigeon dares to dance,
coos an anorexic tune
to play the formal mating game.
He needs such annual fission,
feeds his soul on ritual passion,
treads an ancient wheel.

The blackbird takes such risks
to rear her quiet offspring
– grounded, open to attack
by squirrel, hawk or passing cat:
humble makar, knowing that
her progeny are frail.

We had our share of visitors, like Eric and Sheena Waugh, who were fellow-missionaries – Eric's father had been the beadle in St Michael's Church, Linlithgow, and we had together led the Bible Class for a couple of years there. We entertained Ann Jackson, who served as a doctor in Biafra and saw the horrors of the Nigerian civil war, now largely written out of their history books, though as it happens Handsel Press has just published her war zone journal, *Last Doctor out of Biafra*, in 2019 (edited by Joanna and Will Storrar). We welcomed Howard and Eleanor Taylor, who were then in Malawi; all people whose missionary commitment we hugely admired.

Margaret's father James Munro spent the war in the Seychelles. Having left school age fourteen, he graduated first in his year at Robert Gordon's College in Aberdeen, doing his architectural training. Then while he worked on designing the old Leith Hospital, he met Margaret's mother Peggy in Edinburgh, and eventually took her back to Turriff where he settled into his rural practice.

We have some of his paintings from those days. And some of Margaret's also, when she found the time, usually on holiday. Like the 'summer' we travelled with friends all the way down to Malawi, nappies pinned by the windows to dry in the sun as we drove. There was the car journey ferrying us up the mountain to Livingstonia from Lake Malawi, with only one of our cars able to get up the hill with any extra weight . . . finding that new road without any border post across the hills into Zambia, and being honest enough to try to report to a police station (a bad idea) . . . and finally getting to Dar-es-Salaam to do a locum for a couple of weeks, living in the manse in Chakichaki Street (so called after the noise of the slave chains). In Dar es Salaam she did manage a few paintings.

Border Crossing

How significant
to come across an unmarked
border crossing, pass
from one realm to another,
hear the birds sing just the same.

One letter (no emails then) would prove significant. Professor T.F. Torrance invited me to set up what became the Handsel Press, along with himself, and when we returned that worked out under the chairmanship of Douglas Grant, who also oversaw the Church of Scotland bookshop in the days when it was profitable. Margaret designed the logo.

I was looking after the literature work of the Presbyterian Church of East Africa (P.C.E.A.), writing and teaching a book sometimes in three languages, with the help of my colleague Timothy Ngūmba, and selling these books when we went travelling round the country. Communicating faith is harder in Scotland today than it was then in Kenya. This fact went into a poem about the stones that Joshua set up as a memorial of what God had done (Joshua 4:19-24).

Where are the Stones?

Faith has skipped a generation.
Grandparents try to compensate,
a little desperate, perhaps too late,
but trying, guilt-struck, caring,
mixed up as our world to date.

They wish church stones would speak
a little louder, as stained glass pic-
tures used to. In this new elastic
culture, Facebook, virtual games
and texting mould our plastic

brains, and short term thinking
moves our mental traffic codes
from right to left-brain modes
of practice. Gather living stones,
with faithful story in their lodes.

The polymath Iain McGilchrist describes in his book *The Master and his Emissary* how the West has suffered from giving the left brain, which knows how to get things fixed, priority over the right brain, which deals with goals and with morals. Our milkman, Crispus Kĩongũ, had no need to worry about these European troubles. Crispus was at the time Moderator of the General Assembly, but had a farm near where we lived at Thogoto. He represented the old school. John Gatu, the General Secretary of the P.C.E.A., and later Secretary of the All-Africa Council of Churches, was a forward thinking leader who one day phoned me and invited me to become minister of St Andrew's Church in Nairobi. By that time the P.C.E.A. had had a look at me, and decided they would ordain me in Kiambu Presbytery, where the only other European apart from Margaret was our neighbour Jack Wilkinson, a missionary doctor whose books I was to publish much later, back in Scotland.

I said yes, of course. St Andrews was the old colonial church, where David Steel (now in Linithgow) had been minister. However, the following day, John phoned again and said, "Sorry, the Appointments Committee turned it down". It transpired that the Appointments Committee, led by Crispus Kĩongũ, did not want to lose a missionary serving the church throughout Kenya to a congregation still seen as European (even though by this time it was entirely African).

We spent very little time in Nairobi. Once I agreed to join an ecumenical service in the Anglican Nairobi Cathedral, and found myself giving out the wine at a communion service. I did not know that there it was the custom for the minister to hold the cup to the lips of the communicant, so that he or she did not touch the sacred cup with bare hands; I remember handing a cup full of wine to a Kenyan man – he failed to grasp it, and the wine sloshed all over his lovely suit while I was diving to catch the cup before it hit the deck. I was not asked back.

John Gatu gave the P.C.E.A. the motto *Jitegemea* (self-reliance), and a year later he called for the African Churches to stop relying on overseas missionaries. After much heart-searching, we followed him, rather than Crispus Kĩongũ who was keen for us to stay, and left Kenya after serving there for a little over three years. We were presented with a lovely hand-crafted bag, which I treasured but kept in a cupboard for years, until I remembered it and realised that it really would make a wonderful briefcase.

Briefcase

Twenty years it lay entombed,
a treasure marking time
in a cupboard with no rhyme
or calendar or clock.

Was it a high born antelope,
or humble pig that died,
clean and tidy, to provide
a skin as fine as yours?

The hour has come to resurrect
that life, unlock the door
unblock the memories of yore
that shared the dark with it.

Close up the years, rewind the film,
unstitch the case, unflay
that gorgeous skin, let go and play
the tapes that Kenya holds,

create again the plunging, surging
wildness of a Kenyan plain:
for now its handle fits my skin
I won't forget the life within.

I never forgot Kenya. And the P.C.E.A. did not forget those who had served as missionaries. Today they have several congregations in Britain, and in 2016 they invited us all to Edinburgh for a meal and a service, and said a public thank you. Very moving, not least because they were living proof of how these days Africans are missionaries to European countries whose leaders, in the notorious words of Tony Blair's erstwhile press secretary Alastair Campbell, "don't do God".

Chapter Five

FIRST INTERMISSION – BOAT OF GARTEN

Coming home is seldom easy – returning to a very different culture, and one that was now on the turn, away from holding Christianity as public truth. But that would emerge gradually, in Scotland, as it did earlier in England. We stayed for a while with my mother in Linlithgow, before we moved to our bungalow near Boat of Garten, Millfield (from the local root *Mullin* as in Mullingarroch). We had a great view of the Cairngorms.

Sensory Overload

To see the world, climb half a mile
from Black Park, heading for Whitewell.
Clear your lungs and breathe the view
from Sugar Loaf to Shepherd's Hill.

Adjust your eyes to spot the silence
of millennia, glimpse the waste
of time in noisy city life,
open lips and sharpen taste.

All-round vision – listening birches
sing their notes, unfold their leaves;
even clouds of juniper berries
dance on staves like semibreves.

Fall wind blowing off Braeriach
bent that solitary pine:
touch it, hear those gentle bark scales
bring your senses into line.

The first mountain I climbed was Braeriach, age 12, up over Sron na Lairig; followed by Cairn Gorm – taking bicycles up through the Sluggan Pass to Loch Morlich, and leaving them there to walk up to the summit, years before the new road was built from Coylumbridge, later extended to the ski slopes. Before that it was the Ochils, with Ben Cleuch the highest hill; its height is fixed in my memory, in the old-fashioned measure: 2363 feet.

Why do people climb a mountain? The stock answer is 'because it's there', but I would add that for me (and I often walked alone, which is not always sensible) a mountain is half way between a retreat and a pilgrimage. A time to withdraw and reflect, and a place which is apart. A retreat is typically short, and intense; a pilgrimage is longer, and sweeps up ordinary life into it; both involve the intention to grow in faith and hope and love.

A late friend of mine, Andrew Patterson, nursed his wife for a long time through a terminal illness. He was a minister and a biker, an expert on pilgrimage all over Europe. When she died he went on a special journey, with a canal boat, and I wrote this poem for his own funeral years later.

An Honest Pilgrimage

No need for Chaucer to unleash his scrutiny
of pilgrim motives; no necessity for Bunyan
following up his progress to a city;
here we find a plain and honest man
whom God has taken, dusted down and led
to serve his fellows as a councillor
with honest counsel; humble teacher, well read,
pilgrim biker, then an all-round minister
who earned and learned this trusted role as fighter
for the underdog, a listener, lover
caring to the bitter end, a writer
on the pilgrim way himself – a brother.

So, that slow canal boat journey, thinning
into tunnel dark, is over: now a new beginning.

One of life's many privileges is meeting humble and outstanding people. I think of a younger American couple, Matt and Julie Canlis, who founded the Abbey Summer School, and always included a day of pilgrimage. The first year it was to Inchcolm, in the Firth of Forth. Inchcolm is an island named after St Columba, which was a kind of 'Eastern Iona', later an Augustinian foundation, until raids by the English and the ravages of time made its building a ruin.

Inchcolm

Join the cacophony of gulls, teenagers,
plumage whitening round the neck,
dressing for the dance their elders
choreograph a thousand thousand times
until they drop and join the litter
which infests this trampled island.

Ride the humming wave of tourists
breaking in multi-coloured foam
with a flotilla of footwear, thin
to bear this weight of curiosity;
dark and light-skinned, with a titter
of tongues to probe this listening island.

See through the raggle of styles,
roofs rough stoned and stepped;
a peppering of plaques among the ruins,
an iron ship with sail set for the wind
above the chapter house; a glitter
of sun to fleck this sombre island.

And then:
a genesis of quiet,
an exodus of tourists,
a leviticus of simple ritual,
numbers of unseen guests,
a deuteronomy of something
    rediscovered:
this pentateuch of earth and
    angels,
with somewhere
a memory of holiness.

Inchcolm is very different from the infamous island in the middle of Loch an Eilean, near Aviemore, which was the home of a local brigand, the Wolf of Badenoch. At one time there was a hidden causeway under the water, with a dogleg to trap the uninitiated.

I remember a winter when the loch froze over, and one could walk out to the island. On a calm day the castle is reflected in the water, and offers one of the best echoes in Scotland. Our daughter Elinor was married there – a great day, with occasion to entertain Dutch visitors, put up a gazebo, pipe the bride to the lochside, preach at the wedding (Margaret married the couple), strike the gazebo . . . all before the reception. Church weddings are much simpler!

Boat of Garten was in its own way a place of retreat, and would continue to be so for many years afterwards, not least when it was the only home we owned. At this time we were waiting, wondering what our next part would be – unsure when the film set would move on. Like being stuck on a steam railway, some forty years later in the North York Moors.

Bridge Passage

Life paused a hundred feet above the Esk,
snapped a stream shooting past, the way
these waters slip and slalom. Dark and grey,
the surface quickstepped by, nature brisk
with her own purpose underneath my gaze,
leaving me a voyeur on a tower,
trapped in a train: a sudden loss of power
which seemed to freeze us in a frame for days.

These moments pass; the film set moves again,
each passenger a star in a crowded sky,
a walk-on expert, stepping quick to gain
some purchase on this gifted life, a fly
on God's wall, willing all its tiny brain
to fathom space-time, and eternity.

Perhaps I was doing the searching, and Margaret was doing the waiting, as she was heavily pregnant with our third child Elinor, who would make the Street of Kincardine her home later on in life. Margaret's mother was staying with us to help hold the household together, as I was busy writing a new version of the Church of Scotland Prayer Booklet, then to be called *Pray Today*. In those days adding pictures was the latest thing – the current version has reverted to text.

Writing prayers maybe nudged me subconsciously towards poetry. The boundary between poetry and prose has become more fluid over my lifetime. Modern poetry depends on rhythm more than rhyme, with strict metric forms much less common. But I do not recall thinking these thoughts then; I was thinking about the next step.

In Kenya we had had a visit from David Steel, who was out visiting friends from the days when he himself was minister of St Andrew's, Nairobi. "Jock," he said, "I think you should go to St Cuthbert's." Dr Steel had himself once been associate minister at St Cuthbert's, a big church at the west end of Edinburgh's Princes St, and knew it was coming vacant.

I gritted my teeth, smiled and said very little, not relishing having my career mapped out by such a great fixer as David Steel; later on, his son – Lord Steel – would be known as 'great David's greater son' (parodying the hymn about David and Christ). Sure enough, back in Linlithgow, I was asked to preach in St Michael's so that members of St Cuthbert's vacancy committee could hear me. Naughtily, I preached a hell fire sermon (not my usual) and succeeded in putting them off; instead they called Tom Cuthell, whose family came from Bo'ness.

A 'call' is the decision by a nominating committee conveyed to the minister that they want him or her to be their minister, a decision which must be confirmed by the congregation after the minister has preached as 'sole nominee', and by the Presbytery. Internally, it should be the conviction on both sides that this is the right move.

Bo'ness was where my maternal grandfather lived; he was the superintendent of St Andrew's Church Sunday School, and would always pipe them off on their annual picnic. I never went to Sunday school, but I did lead the Bible Class in St Michael's Church, along with my fellow-student Eric Waugh. Two of the members subsequently got married; we kept in touch, and recently I sent Margaret Henderson, now secretary of the Friends of St Michael's, a poem to celebrate a church anniversary.

A Sonnet at 775

Odd numbers these, much easier to say
this church is seven centuries my elder,
worked out to a year (if not a day).
Each member still a living body builder
of its serious but seldom joyless history,
its dialogue of sermon, stone and song,
celebrating life and gospel mystery,
a standing witness to what's right and wrong,
yet smiling gently on each wondered at newborn,
each wedding dress, each coffinful of grief.
St Michael's, kind to kin and stranger, worn
and frayed by Cromwell, time or other thief,
ring out your bells to make us still aware
of God who even numbers each grey hair.

At that point in time I had no grey hairs, and churches were keen to get young ministers. So another 'plum' congregation wanted to hear me – located just outside Aberdeen, with the biggest Sunday School in that Presbytery; after I had preached they invited Margaret and me to a lavish lunch. I had no sense of call, felt I was there under false pretences, and was very relieved when we all came to the same mind about it.

For that occasion we stayed with Margaret's parents in Turriff. But most of that year we spent at Boat of Garten. Millfield was close to the old Mullingarroch Mill. It was a Dorran bungalow, the last one built before the firm went bankrupt, and it would last well beyond its advertised life of thirty years. Years later I was sitting there looking out of the window, and said to Margaret, "Tell me what to write about." "Birch trees," she said.

Beauty and Bioethics

The oaks and pines, the lines
carved out by glaciers in retreat,
these made our eco-story,
formed and clothed our hills and glens;
their large scale legacy defines

where beauty shows, and goes
to help us write our history, be it
animal or vegetable or mineral,
and understand which trees survive
and which do not. Who knows,

we might now change a range
of likely outcomes, when we plant
a mix of woodland, look at
grazing habits, think of deer
and other animals. Strange

how sheep were grown, condoned
by greedy landlords, bent on driving
out their tenants with the cattle
which had kept the bracken well at bay
and left the trees alone.

Some types survive, and thrive
without the ancient Caledon; the rowan,
alder, sycamore, the hazel,
but the birch outclasses all of them,
my favourite of the five.

As I recall, we all
would run our fingers up and down
the bark, so smooth and silver
to our adolescent touch and see,
then grieve each autumn leaf fall.

The trunks grow fast, and last,
but not for ever. I have watched,
seen them thrust and thicken,
press towards an adult life,
the vagaries of childhood past.

Small aphids hide inside
the canopy, appreciating nature's
hospitality, world wide
web, original internet,
without a human guide.

When old enough, it's rough
to touch, but keeps its silver texture;
shapely summer miracle,
a filigree of perforated green,
lovely, eye-embracing stuff.

The branches host the most
surprising little birds: warblers,
finches, tits; a pheasant
pecks around for seed that falls
from feeders to the ground, engrossed

– and why not? Food is good
for every creature, and we like
to add our titbits to the mix.
Yet mind brings more, can see a tree,
not just some leaves and wood.

For when man came to name
the animals, that was chapter two;
in chapter one, God says,
'Take care of everything – the green
stuff matters just the same.'

The jury's out. About
a dozen species vanish daily.
What kind of minder is the
one which cannot handle climate
change without a doubt?

Vested interests apart, I can think of two reasons why people ignore climate change. It's big, and many people feel it's way beyond them. It's slow, and politicians like to keep their focus on what may happen before the next election. For me it was more satisfying to write a poem about it than to write to an MP who was probably too busy on other things.

For most people 'green stuff' means lettuce and broccoli, rather than tree canopies in a tropical forest. Margaret was always pretty good on diet (her mother was a dietician), while the one thing I used to jump up and down about was porridge. Oatmeal porridge, not porage oats. I used to cook it the way my mother made it, adding some invented mathematics about the height of pouring and the speed of rotation to justify my technique.

Porridge

While I praise the variety, grits to ugali,
my stomach is stern – it must be oatmeal,
and medium at that. Heat water, add salt,
put meal in a mug thin enough you can feel
that your hand's in a claw at a generous height.
Tap tap with a finger, a golden Niagara
must hit boiling water at speed, so the grains
will be shocked to the core, surrender their flavour
by opening their hearts. Your spirtle is stirring
and stirring and stirring, the steam is uprising
and catching the fluff, that finger is rapping
away on the mug till it's void; not surprising
you breathe again, smile at the pot; now the panic
is over, let nature conclude with its magic.

Once we went to Crieff Hydro for a holiday, and I found on the breakfast menu the claim, 'Traditional Scottish Porridge' when porage oats were being served. I complained. On a subsequent visit I found nothing had changed, so I took up the matter with the managing director, Stephen Leckie, pulling rank a little as I used to play in the Crieff Pipe Band with his father. He listened. On my next visit I found the menu simply said 'Scottish Porridge'. Tactful, but not much better.

North of Millfield, nestled on a plateau above Loch Ness, is Moniack Mhor, a creative writing centre which I have visited for courses. It has a marvellous view – from my bedroom window I once counted no fewer than seven different mountain ranges. A walk through a neighbouring forest where timber works had been interrupted led to this poem.

Green Battlefield

To fell, then fail to finish felling,
leaving half a forest naked
to the wind is criminal. Conifers
now are refugees undressed
upon a battlefield, shivering,
fearful, ruined by the halted cut.

The storm was bound to intervene,
and pick off pine trees one by one,
then two by three by four, a column
taken enfilade, a whole battalion killed
and left to decompose in rows
with roots upturned and dead clock faces.

To fall, and feel the air invade
their guts, a pool of water filling
at their wrinkled roots, that fate
is terminal: so, they lie unburied,
warrior giants disarmed and left
uncounted, torn and unlamented.

Beside them, bumble bees now fumble
in the bugle flowers, while grey black
coal tits flock and flash their white,
the young pines sprout their tops
as if no tempest ever raged,
and rowans, myrtle, birch appear.

To fool around with clever words
will not avenge those battle-scars.
Go deeper, ask, what mailed fist
is clenched? And which dark general
lets the gale gun down civilian trees
like this? The air is full of poison.

Crowberry and lichen linger, nature
signals: we can rise to fight again,
and from the moss a thousand tips
rise up, green cotton buds, a model
army ranked and ready for our vote,
our steel gloved poems as antidote.

The path I was walking in Boat of Garten was rather different, and included impending fatherhood. Margaret had been confined to bed for the last stages of pregnancy, until finally I took her up to Raigmore Hospital in Inverness. As we waited by ourselves in a room, sitting beside some old fashioned heating pipes which obviously went round all the buildings, I decided to sing (psalms!) to keep our spirits up – we were on our own – until an embarrassed nurse came in and said, "Please stop, you can be heard all over the hospital!"

It was those pipes of course. Reputations spread in unsought ways. I suppose that was how in the end I got a call to the Steeple Church in Dundee. Professor Jack Martin had come to a course when I was assistant warden of St Ninian's Training Centre, and when he heard I was looking for a church he got some others on the vacancy committee to meet me. Then I preached in St Peter's (now Dundee Free Church) so they could hear me. Nowadays, ministers normally have to apply for churches.

Chapter Six

DUNDEE

Actually it was also a 'deferred call' to the Steeple Church. From April 1976, for the first two years I was the minister of Old St Paul's and St David's united with Wishart Memorial Church, where services were held for the first five weeks. Not far away was the Wishart Arch where the Reformer stood and preached to those sick of the plague, citing Psalm 107:20, "God sent his word and healed them." The people of Dundee initially had no time for George Wishart, but when the epidemic broke out they sent a message asking him to return; he did, he preached, the plague stopped.

Wishart was Mary Slessor's church, the mill girl who became one of the British consuls in Nigeria; had she been a man, she would have been more famous than David Livingstone. As a girl she became a fearless member of a gang consisting till then only of (young) boys, and she became a Christian because she went and listened to an old woman sitting at a fire on the stone floor of a tenement building. The woman pointed to a blazing stick and said, "Unless you believe on the Lord Jesus Christ you will burn in hell like that." Mary changed, dramatically – but in all her missionary work, she never used those hell fire tactics herself.

Our first service coincided with the clocks going forward by one hour. We had just arrived, were not well organised, and providentially on the

Sunday morning someone phoned and said, "Are you remembering . . . ?" We rushed down to church and got there just in time.

It was a dramatic start, not least because in the first few weeks a member of the Boys Brigade came to me and said that the captain had been abusing him while they were away at camp. We were naïve in those days, and expressions like child protection and safeguarding had not been invented. I simply summoned the captain, told him I wanted his resignation immediately, and got it. Nearly fifty years later, out of the blue I got a phone call from the Dundee Social Work Department asking about it, as the police were now involved; I really struggled to remember the details. Getting justice after such a passage of time is important, but not easy.

Wishart Memorial Church was now facing closure. I remember going up to Roy Hogg, then minister of the High Church, and saying, "Roy, if you had a redundant church, what would you do with it?" Quick as a flash he replied, "I would give it to Dundee Cyrenians." So we did, and I became chair of the Cyrenians, I suppose partly out of a sense of responsibility to see that it was used properly.

It was, of course, not least because people like Sam Will were involved. Sam was a retired Free Church missionary in Peru, and I still remember his words, "I'm coming to the finishing straight of my life, and I want to give it all I've got!"

Sam Will

Sam Will, Sam Will, and willing indeed
to live and lead from head to toe,
to serve where others would not go,
Sam Will, Sam Will, and willing still.

Sam Will, Sam Will, and willing he was
to lead because he heard the call
to leave his homeland, serve with all
his heart and mind, his art and skill.

Sam Will, Sam Will, and willing his friends
to make amends to those in need,
to join him where he went to feed
the homeless, house them, pay the bill.

Sam Will, Sam Will, and willing indeed
to pay good heed, no matter what
it took to give them all he'd got;
Sam Will, Sam Will, Sam always will.

Years later I visited Peru with the Vine Trust, and met Paul Clark, legendary for his work with street children. I heard how Sam Will had once stood on a beach in South America with a crowd watching a doctor trying to come ashore in a small boat. The boat capsized in a heavy sea. Sam took charge, getting people to form a human chain on a rope so they could bring the man safely in. With him on the beach was young Paul, who dates his call to 'rescue work' from that experience.

Another stalwart of Dundee Cyrenians was Sheriff Graham Cox. It was a standing joke that he would be in the night shelter of an evening with the same people who would be up before him on some charge or other the following day. In those days, work among the homeless was typically confined to running a night shelter – but acquiring a church building let us start a Day Centre, which later included a city farm. Among other benefits, this gave homeless men something to do as well as somewhere to go during the day. One such was John McKay.

Was it a goat
or ghost I saw on the pavement,
attached to John, proud street walker
of the city farm menagerie
that flitted through the annals of Dundee?

McKay he was,
but English to the core, loyal
to Her Majesty, whose guest he was
from time to time, as Christmas
on the street's for sheep, not goats.

He had an eye,
indeed a gift for demolition,
better channelled against masonry
than men, and great free labour
for the voluntary sector.

The law's an ass,
but with a goatish sense of humour
gifted John McKay two years of travel
round the world, as compensation
for some rather nasty pokery.

I see his ghost
still tending animals who scented
tenderness in his odd corners.
I bless the goats who do the things
that faithful sheep might fail to do.

John had indeed a gift for demolition, which we used well enough in the other church when its turn came for closure, and in the city centre flat we developed. But he had his enemies, and the poem above refers to an occasion when a poker was rammed up his anus, which allowed him to claim Government compensation. He also had his soft side, a love for animals.

In Dundee we acquired a dog – a bitch, to be accurate, a beagle whose pedigree name Kittoch Bonnet we shortened to Bo. One evening we went out to see the film 'Ghandi' in a small cinema in the Hilltown, leaving a student to babysit. Half-way through the film there was an interruption, and a stewardess came and found us – can you imagine that in a cinema today? We were told that our babysitter had locked himself out of the manse. We went home, let him in, and discovered a cat's cradle up and down stairs – Bo had found a ball of red wool and chased it round the house.

Like many young dogs, Bo was not fussy about her diet, which one day included our album of wedding photos. The next day, clearly wanting to communicate, she chewed a game called 'Sorry'.

A Gospel for Dogs

'Follow the light you have, and pray for more'
– George MacLeod

She follows the light, and prays for some more,
the light of a fridge and a wide open door,
the sight of a friend collecting a lead,
though a walk comes second in line to a feed.
She thinks with her stomach and talks with her tail,
stolen liver and bacon's the most holy Grail;
where food's unattended, she's first at the feast
– well, mercy's essential for both man and beast.

Being a city centre minister brought me in touch with some extraordinarily gifted people. Andy Thornton was my assistant for a year, a wonderful guitar player who went on later to be the administrator for Greenbelt Festival. He and Ricky Ross joined Alan Torrance, Jeremy Begbie, David Heavenor and myself on a mission to my old School, Sedbergh. Alan and Jeremy went on to become professors of theology, David is a songwriter on the staff of the Queens Hall in Edinburgh, Ricky stayed around his home town of Dundee for a while before he became lead singer of Deacon Blue, and now a broadcaster.

Ricky was also my pastoral assistant for a year. At that point, Church of Scotland was a good half-way house between the Brethren assembly where he was brought up, and the Roman Catholic church to which he currently belongs. Ricky led our church theatre company, and I recall an outstanding performance of *The Glass Menagerie*. He was in charge of the Slessor Youth Project, which funded over twelve people through Urban Aid. I rather thought he was wasted going into pop music...

In 1977 the Riding Lights Theatre Company was founded by Paul Burbridge and Murray Watts in York. I was asked to be a trustee, which was about the time that Murray and I first met. Later I was to become chair of the Wayfarer Trust, which supports the work that Murray does with artists and writers from many countries. Murray thrives on adventure, one of his biggest being the purchase of Freswick Castle, a wonderful but ruined Viking site in the far north east of Scotland.

The Garden at Freswick Castle

No blandscape here, no empty atmosphere:
from gappy outhouse doors swallows appear,
swoop and sweep lines round invisible canvas;
bluebells gently peer from fine green ferns,
grey juniper rises, yawns and hunkers down.

Daffodils upon the edge are tall, full on,
their town-bound cousins fallen, dead and gone;
a wren is singing, loudly telling peewits
and the plovers 'small is beautiful';
ochre lichen creeps along the stone.

Years ago that wall was built, set low:
flat-laid monument of place, and slow,
slow hours, full of the grass in the garden;
crow-stepped pigeons perch on lazy minutes,
every second soft with the sound of the sea.

Wayfarer is an arts charity, and in any recession, arts funding is usually the first to be cut and the last to recover. Bodies who give money often prefer projects to core funding, which in some cases has led to imaginative things happening, but in other cases has led bodies doing great ongoing work to tie themselves in knots trying to invent projects which can carry some core funding on the back of a 'project'.

My time in Kenya had awakened me to the impact which politics (as well as the arts) could have on the lives of ordinary people. Our local MP was Gordon Wilson, then one of the few SNP MPs. But actually Dundee Presbytery was responsible for my warming to the idea of Scottish independence – a far cry from the taken-for-granted unionism in which I was brought up. Presbytery organised what nowadays we would call a hustings, with speakers from Labour, Conservative, Liberal and SNP, invited to talk on 'the moral and spiritual aspects of devolution'.

The SNP guy was the only one of the four who addressed the subject, and who did not spend the time slagging his opponents' views. I suddenly realised I should think about this. My problem was that for me Christian faith was international; I had many English friends, and I did not want to support something that would be bad for my English neighbours.

After two weeks of cogitation I had recognised three reasons why Scottish independence might be good for England also:

- The Scottish tradition was to vest authority in 'the people' rather than 'the Parliament', and this, I thought, was a sounder European tradition which England should be faced with.

- England (at that time) had no clear sense of national identity – people belonged, for example, to Yorkshire and Britain – and they would be better off developing their own sense of identity.

- Because Scotland was always shouting the odds, the peripheral and poor areas like Northumberland and Cornwall were being neglected; if Scotland were no longer part of UK, then England would be better placed to address its own issues of poverty and inequality.

A few years later I was at a family party when a cousin casually said to me, "Jock, you've been a minister for a while – isn't it time you went into politics?" Rather a strange remark, I thought at the time. Indeed, while I regard politics as an important calling, I had no doubt that I was in the right place myself, and that politics could become a kind of idolatry as much as anything else.

Wealthy Nation

Left and Right: two feet that kick their targets
wealth and poverty, sloganning a nation stuck
in apathy, despair or affluent ipaddery
(offering mirages and their virtual riches) –
depending where and when you push your luck
as poet, commentator or observant citizen.
Light twitterers and heavy letter writers
plunge their virtual pens into the ruck,
cherry picking Adam Smith or Robert Burns,
citing innovators, quoting wise and foolish,
whether Kerevan or Fry or even Friar Tuck
who, remember, had a fairly moral take
on wealth, as did the great economist
so glibly mentioned out of context. Muck
and brass no longer meld: that Scotland
saw its coal and steel and heavy jobs
that built great merchant houses come unstuck
and leave us vulnerable. No single vision
grips the minds and heads of those who,
losing God, can only blindly pass the buck
to mortal characters like May or Sturgeon.
Come back, true poverty of spirit, offering us
a wealth of wisdom which will never duck
the questions we should put to Left and Right.

When that poem was first written, it was 'Cameron or Salmond', not 'May or Sturgeon', and now it will need further updating.

I never doubted that all Parties contained men and women who wanted the best for their country. One of our elders was Johnny Johnston: district secretary of the Transport and General Workers Union – in those days I could have written T.G.W.U. and everyone would recognise the initials – and a hard worker. Later on, however, he was to give me a warning: he had always told himself that when he retired he would spend more time with his wife, but when she died before him he realised that it was too late. "Don't you go and make the same mistake!" he told me.

One thing I tried to do was 'read' the city. It was John Maxwell, known as 'the tailor of Dundee', who told me I must read the book *Witches' Blood*, which tells the story of the city from the underside, against 'the right ones' who ran the Church and the Council.

Recently I was invited back to write and discuss a poem connecting another book, *Moving Towards Emmaus*, by David Smith, which is an extended reflection on Luke 24:13-35, two men on a journey to Emmaus joined by a mysterious figure who breaks bread in their home and is recognised as the Christ.

Back to the City

"It's so easy to get out of, Dundee!" folk said,
putting on a victim habit. As so many did:
Wishart, driven out at first for preaching,
called back in to ban the plague; Annan,
sailing for America, shipwrecked, ruined,
lost and found, rough diamond drowned
to save a lad in trouble in the River Tay;
Slessor, leaving loom and weaving room
for Africa, and with that a place in history;
Galloway and Cox, Ross and Kelly moving out
to seek a freshly coloured page, a bigger stage.
Are we leavers, on for off, all the way down?

"We kept hoping for better", they said
right through the decades of corruption,
as one does when leaders take their cash
tax-free in plain brown envelopes. That
post-war period, full of messianic claims
which shrivelled on the stony path of progress.
"Better what?" a traveller ought to ask,
"What makes a city good to live in, good
to die in?" Have ideals dried up and died
behind the back of urban and suburban sofas?
Can we start to share our loss and pain
before we mutter words of hope again?

"It had to be this way", he said, "Didn't it?"
A question from beyond, heuristic, carried
them from Dundee to Emmaus. Witches Blood
does not exhaust a city, for a deeper magic
is at work; Christ treads upon the water,
not of Lake Tiberias, but Tay; and we sense
companion footsteps all along the Nethergate.

Fate and freedom tussle for supremacy,
but he walks through our philosophy
unrecognised, yet listening to our questions;
when we're ready, he might well explain
us to ourselves, and give our city commentary.

"Stay with us", they told him, "Come inside,
relax, and join us at the supper table."
So he did, and when they shared their food
one spell was cast, another broken with the bread;
a couple passed into our precious stories:
epiphany at eating time, a holy hospitality.
Come back, George Wishart, now we recognise
your testimony. Come right back, Ma Slessor,
with your children; we can now embrace
the refugee adventurers from every race.
Come back, rough Robert Annan, bring
your gospel courage, transformation, everything.

"We're going back", they told each other, "right
back to the city." Then, make an urban garden,
grow flowers out of concrete, farm the city green,
look out for the stranger, follow Wedderburn
and make a godly ballad to reform this age.
Lift the Topaz from McGonagall, the McIntosh
from Patrick, weave a kilt of colour round the Broons.

Partner with your purpose, dance into the future,
for the past is sorted and its weight of evil thwarted,
bloodline clean; now powers at work unseen
encourage us to cancel leave, baptize the nitty-gritty
and be spiritual pace-makers, heart-beat of our city.

Magic has long been banished from the western world, or so we think. I brought a lovely Makonde carving home from East Africa, and for a year or two it was parked in our manse. I knew it was supposed to be a representation of the devil, and one day a visitor challenged me, "What is the devil doing in your house?" Now, the founder of the Salvation Army would have sold it for a large sum and "washed the money in the tears of widows and orphans", but I simply took the carving out of the parish and put it into a workmen's brazier to be consumed.

Makonde Magic

Beautifully made, but somewhat devilish
with those eyes, or breasts, or bumps
of smooth Makonde magic, a glimpse
below the surface of a world view,
fifth column on the watch, awake; a cuckoo
flown from Tanzania to a different parish.

I thought no more about this kind of thing until we had a visit from the Healing Minister George Fox. He was holding a service in our church, and he was not seeing the response he normally saw elsewhere. George was uneasy; at the close he asked me, "Is there anything in the area behind me which ought not to be there?"

I immediately thought about the big brass plate we were using to collect offerings, right behind where he was standing. When the congregations united in the Steeple Church, I had wanted to bring in one or two items from the other churches. Wishart Church had a collection of memorabilia from the days of Mary Slessor, and this brass plate from Nigeria was one of the items.

I said nothing about the plate to him, but asked if he would wait a minute in the vestry. I then quietly removed the plate, and asked him to come back into the church. At once he said, "Oh, things are all right now!"

Make of that what you will. Later I took the plate along to the Dundee Museum and asked what the carving on it was. "That's a carving of a river goddess – nice piece of work." I did not tell anyone what I had done – I was a little embarrassed, to be honest – but I gave the plate to the Museum.

A highlight of our ten years in the city was a mission which an Augustinian friar, Larry Brassill and I found ourselves leading. The Roman Catholic bishop was old, and it was the time of Charismatic Renewal, so that things were possible then which sadly do not happen today. We invited Cardinal Suenens over from Belgium as our missioner, Protestants and Catholics shared communion, and about a hundred young people made a commitment and were followed up by different congregations.

I had a discussion with Suenens about the future of the Christian Church in Europe. He said to me enthusiastically, "It won't be very long before we'll be one Church!" I thought at the time, and even more so now, that he was over-optimistic . . . but then, the Roman Catholic Church thinks in centuries, while we think in years.

I recall a visit by a young Catholic nun to talk to people in our congregation. Suddenly she stopped mid-flow, turned to a young student in the front row, and said, "You have a beautiful face." Then she continued with her talk. It was an example of a prophetic 'word from God'. That student was deeply touched, grew in self-confidence, completed her training to become a doctor, and made a happy marriage.

A city centre church is typically blessed with people from many places. One of our younger members was Zedi Nyirenda, later a civil engineer in London, then in his home country of Malawi. his wife Jo worked for the British Council. We ordained Zedi as an elder.

When Old St Paul's and St David's Church was closed, it became the Mary Slessor Centre, nowadays hosting a youth project called 'Hot Chocolate'. For a while it was empty, and with people like Ricky Ross and Andy Thornton around, it was no surprise that we launched a city centre festival, called Street Level, which featured a young John Bell, a young Sally Magnusson, a young Adrian Plass, and (of course) the Bogle Band. It was good for the city to see a church humming, and good for the congregation to meet such interesting people.

John Bell is known worldwide as a church musician, but is today equally used as a speaker and consultant. Years later I was at a poetry retreat high up at Los Olivos in the Spanish Sierra Nevada, and found myself occupying a room John had occupied the week before. Off the room was a little square, enclosed monk's cell with a roof open to the sky, where I wrote this poem:

Chimney to the Sky

I sit at a computer,
and forget the great Sierra circling me.
I sit in a square chimney,
three white walls, a door, a roof of sky.

I sit at a computer,
and write of every day, companions
perching in Los Olivos,
nesting, trusting that an egg or two
may hatch some wisdom
bringing out the warmth we seek
from life's strange fires.

I sit at a computer, and the mountains
give me hospitality;
I scramble up my chimney to the sky.

Los Olivos was run until 2018 by two men who are now married to one another, one an Episcopal minister – an event which was unheard of in my Dundee days. Events like Street Level crossed many boundaries, but not that one.

One of the boundaries in student life was between the Christian Union branches and the Student Christian Movement branches. The SCM dates from 1889, and the division started just after the First World War, when students in several universities began forming Christian or Evangelical Unions which in 1928 came under the umbrella of what is now the Universities and Colleges Christian Fellowship (UCCF). This could lead to what others might call turf wars, and one year I was asked to chair a meeting between the two bodies, to help them reach agreement on how to avoid conflict in the way they presented themselves to students.

Fixing one's own boundaries is hard for those in the caring professions. We kept an open home, which led to us having a recovering drug addict for one spell. There were a good many others who lived with us for periods – one was Christine Ramsden, from my old Sheffield connections, who later became a deaconess in the Church of Scotland. I confess that for me these were 'projects', whereas for Margaret, with our three children Dorothy, Katherine and Elinor to look after as well, it was a heroic piece of service which I did not fully appreciate at the time. She herself, as a natural carer, would always find it hard to set her own boundaries – and at this point I was little help to her. I was behaving like Richard Holloway, who describes in his autobiography *Leaving Alexandria* how during his time as rector of Old St Paul's Church in Edinburgh he would escape to his study, leaving his wife Jean to deal with the bustle.

I had a habit of getting up early to read the Bible – an excellent habit, one I am grateful for. But I had a key lesson to learn. At the start of our married life I could not understand why Margaret found it so hard to get up early; coming from a family of larks, I was not used to the ways of owls; nor did I understand that if Margaret stayed in bed in the morning, it was because that was the only quiet space she could find for her own devotions. I was critical of her, until I learned to be critical of myself.

By this time we had moved into the Steeple Church after a couple of years in Old St Paul's and St David's Church. It became a refuge for people from all denominations, though I recall a conversation without animosity where I had to advise one of our members to attend another congregation because she really wanted 'traditional Church of Scotland', and we didn't do that. I headhunted an organist, Neville Simpson, who had left the Church of Scotland because it was too dull, and was playing euphonium in a Salvation Army band. He was a great organist, but not gifted with choirs, so we agreed that I organise the singers and he play the organ. Gradually we removed the pews from the back of the church to make room for refreshments, sound desk and things of that kind – but recently the whole church building has had a thorough makeover, returning the 'pulpit' and table to a long wall, opposite where it originally was, long before our time.

The Steeple Church

Easy to make out, in fact,
no need for any fiction,
and as for making up,
that's in the job description.

Make for it past the penguins,
you'll make it in a trice,
no need for make-believe
or made up artifice.

It's made of faith and history,
make of that what you will;
but come to making over
– that cost over a mill.

I became Presbytery Finance Convener in succession to Professor Jack Martin, from whom I learned always to soften people up with a joke before you hit them with figures. Once I reported back from a conference with a suggestion to reform the Presbytery. They appointed me convener of a committee to do just that. When we did report, it took a whole year to debate the recommendations. We thought we had won a few battles, but (greenhorn that I was) we lost the war because I failed to get the right reforming people chosen to implement the reforms agreed – so they crumbled.

During our time at the Steeple, the Handsel Press was growing its portfolio of books published, including Lesslie Newbigin's commentary on John's Gospel, *The Light Has Come* (which he himself thought was his most important book). I got my first experience of editing, *Ministers for the '80s* looking at some issues which are coming home to roost in the Church of Scotland today.

We also began to publish booklets on contemporary issues and other subjects. When I look back on the range of authors I have two feelings: amazement at the willingness of so many outstanding people to contribute (see Appendix), and shame that there were no women – it would be so different today.

The Steeple Church is at one end of the 'City Churches' complex in the Overgate. Originally full of people living in tenements, the area has been redeveloped, and features like a line of bronze penguins have recently been added. Our parish included the old harbour, home to RRS Discovery, HMS Unicorn, and from 2018 the Victoria and Albert Museum of Design. The seafront is extremely busy, but I did manage to find a little bit of water once to conduct two adult baptisms in the sea.

Half way through our time in Dundee, we began to wonder when Margaret would be able to join me in a team ministry. We decided to 'put out a fleece' (which refers to a story about Gideon in the Book of Judges) – we said to God, if this is the right time, let three different people talk to us about Margaret getting ordained (i.e. becoming a practising minister). Sure enough, all three came along very shortly: first the session clerk, David Stibbles, then the student mentioned at few pages earlier, and finally a trainee deaconess (her married name is Liz Crocker). From that time on we have worked together as a team. Some married couples find that difficult – in our case it has probably been easier because our gifts are different and complementary: I am stronger on preaching and administration, Margaret is stronger on visiting and counselling.

This was an issue at national level too. Dundee Presbytery asked us to take an 'overture' to the General Assembly asking approval for married couples to share a stipend. You would think this was easy, but the then secretary of the Dept. of Ministry sent me a shirty letter saying more or less that it would happen over his dead body. Happily, he only had to retire before the Assembly later passed the issue on the nod.

One of the booklets I am glad to have published is *The Ministry of Women*, by T.F. Torrance. It came out in 1992, when the debate in the Church of England was in full swing. On its cover it has a representation of a celebration of communion in 'the Catacomb of Priscilla'; in the original wall painting, Priscilla and Aquila (mentioned in the book of Acts) are presiding together. This is how Margaret had always understood ministry, and I was happy to affirm it.

Someone once asked me whether I enjoyed 'playing a role'. I found it a strange question, as I don't think of myself as a different person in the pulpit from how I am at home. On reflection, I realise some ministers must think of it that way, which for me would be stressful, like acting a part in a play. For me it is just 'who I am'. I enjoy holidays, of course, but I have never thought to retire from 'being a minister'. Another angle is that for me, it is baptism and commitment that make a Christian, not ordination. I certainly don't think of ordained ministry as 'superior' to any other calling.

Being a minister, however, does allow you a marvellous range of contact with people and activities. Near the end of our time in Dundee, in 1985, was the International Year of Youth (2018 is the latest one). I was asked by the Church of Scotland nationally to arrange a festival to celebrate it. One Step Beyond we called it, and I suppose it was a cross between Street Level and what became the Carberry Festival, with many of the same suspects performing on stage, in the South Inch, Perth. We produced a new songbook, the music copy beautifully hand written by our organist.

I seldom fall out with church musicians, but George McPhee and I did disagree about one thing. He was appalled that I should want to resolve the tune Bonny George Campbell to finish the last verse of 'Thank you, O Lord for the time that is now' on the keynote instead of the leading note. With hindsight he had a point – for a festival such as One Step Beyond, it might have been appropriate to end a song 'unfinished', because there is always more to come. But that is a theological point, and George was more interested in the music.

When the time came for us to leave Dundee, the Presbytery Clerk, Mr Bremner, was not pleased. It's a shame you are leaving the ministry, he said. A back-handed compliment, I suppose.

Chapter 7

CARBERRY

Bill Shannon, my old boss at St Ninian's Centre in Crieff, was now convener of the National Mission Committee of the Kirk. One day he came to Dundee and met me in the city centre. As we were driving out to the manse, he said, "How would you like to run Carberry Tower?"

We agreed, but had to keep it under wraps for a year, as we were not ready to leave the Steeple so soon. Even our children did not know – it would have been unfair to ask them to keep a secret like that. In the interim we got an approach from Jack Cumming, interim moderator at Greenbank Church (who had married us), but we had to say we were already committed. Later we would meet their Bible Class, as well as their older youth group Q2, at Carberry Tower, and recently led a retreat there at the invitation of their new minister Martin Ritchie.

Carberry Tower was gifted to the Church of Scotland by the Elphinstone Family in 1951, and the Church also bought the estate (the lawns were knee deep in grass at the time). The Department of Parish Education took on responsibility for its use and upkeep, running it primarily as a Youth Training Centre although also holding courses for bodies such as the National Coal Board and Ferranti.

By the time we were asked, the Church had had one of its internal fights. When Colin Day retired as warden, the Parish Education Committee got East Lothian Council interested in buying Carberry Tower, so they could use the money to set up a Centre beside St Colm's College – but when they took the plan to the General Assembly, the Assembly said no, and added, "If you don't want to run Carberry, we'll find someone else who will." A number of options, including the YMCA, were explored, but in the end the Department of National Mission agreed to run the centre, while it remained in the ownership of the Board of Parish Education.

Carberry Tower was an oasis between Midlothian and East Lothian. It had been the home of the then Queen Mother, a 14th century keep extended over the years, with an estate planted as an arboretum by the Elphinstone family. My hobby on days off was to identify every single tree in the grounds, which I finally completed with the help of George Anderson of the Royal Botanic Garden in Edinburgh, later of Beechgrove Garden fame.

Meantime, our Kate was agitating to get a pony. She had already been to the pet shop, got hold of a cat, and then pretended she had found a stray so that we took pity on it and allowed her to keep it – a stratagem she admitted some 20 years later. But a horse was another kettle of fish, so to speak. Before Bill Shannon spoke to me, I had a killer reply: "If we lived in the country you could have a pony, but we can't keep one in the town" – words which very soon came back to bite me.

Carberry was temporally in the hands of Paul Burgess, formerly a missionary in Pakistan, who had been appointed by Parish Education to run the place down to closure, but who decided to develop the courses instead. He and his wife Cathie stayed on for a couple of years, and we began to get volunteers coming from abroad, many from Hungary. At Christmas we ran a houseparty, at which I made the porridge. Here is another porridge poem, recalling my mother.

Tradition and Technique

I need a pouring Niagara,
a stream of grain
to smack the surface,
diving through the steam
that filters the fluff
and sends it skyward.

Still,
I need to follow how she did it,
ignorant of particle physics,
never-travelled to Ontario,
but well versed in porridge making;
taking salt and Scottish water,
oatmeal from Ann McDonald's mill
let me craft a culinary poem.

It also recalls Ann McDonald, a Guildswoman with clout which she used unstintingly in favour of Carberry, as did Gordon Hector, then secretary to what was later the Assembly Council, whose daughter Katy and her husband Alistair became regular visitors. Ann's family used to have an oatmeal mill at Alford.

At our first Carberry Christmas, Paul Burgess presented me with a large square box wrapped up in Christmas paper. Inside was an Amstrad computer, our first. Soon the time came to equip the office with computers. David Pullinger was at that time working as Society, Religion and Technology Officer for the Church of Scotland; David was a polymath who started his career as a professional French horn player, and even now was director of music at St Paul's and St George's Church in Edinburgh in his spare time. Later in life he chose to work with the National Statistics Office because, he said, it gave him access to Number Ten and the chance to influence Government policy!

The first thing David did, when we asked him for advice, was to sit down with all the office staff, find out how we wanted to use computers, and discuss with us how it would change the way we did things, and how we all felt about that. He knew that computers were there to serve people, not the other way round.

We had marvellous staff, who all became friends – over our time Betty Marshall, Agnes Llano, Margaret Hood and May Kerr served as secretaries or office managers, all from East Lothian. Ailsa McIntyre was in charge of youth work and later married catering manager Ken MacLean, who was from Lewis; there was Marcus Ford, whose father was once a politician in Belize, and so many others. Kathleen Hughes whose husband Clifford became minister of St Mary's Haddington was our house manager for many years. After an operation, Clifford – who had once been a professional lyric tenor – had to use a voice box, with a new career going round hospitals demonstrating how it could be used; he wrote this limerick about himself, including his nickname from when he was in an Oxbridge student choir:

> A tenor called Hairy McKnees
> used to soar to top C's with great ease;
> but his laryngeal 'op'
> caused his voice range to drop
> to basso profundo low D's.

Providentially, although we had to live in the Tower itself for a year, the house we did get to live in had a stable – so we called it The Stables, and it housed a pony. By the time we left Carberry, our second daughter had launched her career as the artist Kate Philp, and did a water colour painting of The Stables which was presented to us.

Our policy of redeveloping the Elphinstone Wing for a residential community allowed National Mission to sell the house Colin Day had lived in, but that set up another conflict – who would get the money, Parish Education or National Mission? Happily, just before it went to a fight on the floor of the Assembly, both parties agreed to share 50-50 . . . and the house then sold for twice its estimated value, so everyone was satisfied.

Charles Spence, who owned the Biel Estate, knew all about property and was a great enthusiast for Carberry. He had head-hunted our factor David Lunn, and like myself believed in doing what needed to be done and asking the committee later on – which worked beautifully for the first few years we were at Carberry, and enabled us to see the whole of the Elphinstone Wing restored to lived-in dwellings, plus a home for what is now Health Link 360.

In 1986, a conference called 'Acts 86' was planned to take place in Birmingham. Through János Pásztor, a colleague from Kenya days, we knew of a number of Hungarian pastors who wished to come, but the then Communist regime would not allow whole groups to go abroad – so we arranged for six of them to stay with families in Edinburgh, and spend some days at Carberry, before going on together to Acts 86. The next year we got invited back to Hungary, so the whole family travelled by car. That led in turn to our daughter Dorothy going for a gap year in 1988 to study music at the Liszt Academy High School.

While we were at Carberry, Dorothy got to know Francis Ogilvy, whose family (by marriage) once owned Biel. Later they got married. There is a more recent fascinating Biel connection. In 1993 the Jesuit House of Study in Dublin became aware through the curator of the National Gallery of Ireland that a painting they had been given around 1930 as a Honthorst was in fact a Caravaggio. This painting had been in the possession of Francis's great, great aunt, Mrs Mary Hamilton Ogilvy of Biel, and when she died in 1920, having been offered to the National Gallery of Scotland under the terms of her will and turned down since they already had a Honthorst, Francis' grandfather sold it at auction for 8 guineas in 1921, then for 5 guineas in 1922, and was later presented to the Jesuits as a thank offering by Dr Marie Lea-Wilson. An offering which turned out to have priceless value.

A painter of a very different kind was Clive Nicholas. Formerly a member of a rocket development team in Australia, he was working for Edinburgh University when he suffered a severe stroke, from which he made an extraordinary recovery, to the extent that although he had to hum rather than speak he became a well-known, saintly, figure at Carberry, which he loved and found to be a healing place. Clive began to paint icons, one of which I still have above my desk, and I wrote this poem for his funeral in 2017:

A Different Life

As the icon painter bares his soul,
wears waistcoat unbuttoned
so God's air can touch his heart,
thus Clive lived his second life.

While the saint kept waiting, shirt
wagered on the fact of God,
so we watched that inner light
grow bright behind his eyes.

And as the world just sometimes
notices a quiet man, humming
a different kind of tune, so
we found extraordinary blessing.

Before getting married I had a policy of living on what I earned, and giving away the income from money I had inherited. Margaret endorsed this policy after we got married, though there were some years when we cheated a little. In Dundee our family were educated in the State sector, but moving to Edinburgh brought a problem: our local school could not offer the same subjects as Morgan Academy in Dundee. (A community can cope with a small private sector without State schools suffering, but in Edinburgh things were different.) In the end we resolved that the children would each receive enough money to give them a good education, and enough for them each to buy a house – so the rest I was able to give away or put into the Charitable Trusts I set up. I have always respected the example of John Wesley, who died leaving £33 and some silver teaspoons, though I cannot claim the same level of obedience . . . nor have I had the opportunity to do my reading on horseback travelling round the country, as he did.

Simple Ambition

I want a future without plastic,
I want to dodge those fleeing shuttles
to a refuge planet, on the front line
of our chic technique and technospeak.

I want a future in the quiet coach,
no fevered fracking this and that;
sweep away derivatives, and complex
economic models, capers that encroach

on who we really want to be.
Give me just one, or two or three
quite simple changes for a better world.
I want a politics that speaks for me.

I want to hear the groaning earth's request
to pause, and heal, and find itself again.
I want to see the evening and the night
bring sleep, and time to love and rest.

But I have no lingering Luddite lust
for fake simplicity, for costly Innisfree.
I'm tired of email spears appearing,
peppering me with ought and must.

I shall simply live the present, loved and fed,
learning, savouring the journey on to Ithaka,
knowing what I give away might somehow
stuff a downie covering a future bed.

While Innisfree is Yeats' mythical island, Ithaka is the home of Odysseus, and Cavafy wrote about the journey to Ithaka, all these great poems are about the importance of the journey itself. We were on a new journey, and we didn't know just where it would take us. We certainly valued our friends and companions.

The Woman's Guild were very supportive, raising enough money to build Guild House which provided essential *en suite* rooms, and because this was a Guild Project we had a stream of Guilds visiting in the summer – up to ten at once, which involved a military style operation moving people from hall to tour to meal to chapel; it worked brilliantly provided the buses were on time. One of those Guild Weeks was particularly busy, and we got a phone call from Chuck Wright in America – Chuck had been at Carberry in connection with the National Prayer Breakfast. "We feel we should be praying for you extra hard this week," he said. "Well," replied Margaret, "we do have 1,300 Guildswomen coming!"

Leading a Centre like Carberry allows one to meet outstanding men and women from all over – we had visits from Eugene Peterson, author of *The Message*, Jean Vanier, founder of L'Arche Community, the missionary statesman Lesslie Newbigin; August Pokorny, director of the Austrian Bible Mission, who before his conversion was a Nazi Youth Leader; John Bell, Michele Guinness, Stewart and Carol Henderson, Adrian Plass, Owen Dudley Edwards, Elisabeth Kübler-Ross, Alex Salmond and so many others. John Stott and John Wimber once held a private breakfast at Carberry to discuss their different approaches.

One of the dangers of leadership is elitism, however (not that any of these people could be described as 'luvvies'). Each person who came to Carberry was important, each member of staff mattered. To keep that focus was a daily challenge, especially when my head was full of planning concerns. Margaret was of course supremely good at this – indeed she generally wore the pastor's hat, while I wore the business hat.

As we continued old courses, and developed new ones, on looking back I think three ventures were the most important:

The Carberry Festival

As well as being an arts festival with vibrant worship, this was a place where families met, friendships grew, and long afterwards, people would return to get married in the chapel. It was modelled on the Dundee Street Level Festival, and in 2017 there was a 30th birthday celebration of the Festival in the Steeple Church in Dundee.

Here is a poem from the book which I launched on that occasion.
I suppose it's an example of what I like to call 'prophetic poetry',
poems which consider social and political issues – maybe dangerous
territory for a minister, but in line with the Old Testament prophets.
Jeremiah was a prophet who was considered a traitor because he said
the Babylonian enemies of Israel were going to overrun Jerusalem and
the whole country. He was in prison, but got the chance to buy a piece
of land, which he did because he wanted to give the people a sign that
in the end, free commerce would be restored to the nation after the
time of God's judgment. In the meantime, those who would shortly be
exiled to Babylon should put down roots there.

Read the Signs

Jeremiah 32.6-12

A straight screw finds a pass
for Jeremiah's cousin Hanamel,
and a bolt snaps somewhere,

giving easy prison access
to a lawyer named Baruch.
Witnesses turn up on time.

The deed is signed – events
then take their crooked path
and creep or stride into our lives

with unexpected consequence
for good and ill, prophetic
elbows nudging us each day.

She fills in forms politely,
clicks them through a second time;
the migrants put down roots

in Babylon or Britain; still,
there's someone stubborn ploughing
hope into the ground back home.

A seed is carried in the flood,
buddlejas wave at passing trains,
fans still follow Cowdenbeath.

The bruised finger retrieves the ring,
distressed flats are clad again,
Americans keep going to the polls.

*The boy puts down a stone, seeing
the ancient tree roots crack a wall;
somewhere a prophet buys a field.*

The arts have many important but overlooked functions in society. One of them is to give people signs of judgement and signs of hope – signs of judgement when people don't see what is rotten, and signs of hope when people have understood the rotten and can't see beyond it.

We had a marvellous team of people organising the Festival. According to Albert Bogle, later to be Moderator of the General Assembly, that team was a model for later ventures like the annual Assembly Celebration 'Heart and Soul' in Edinburgh's Princes St Gardens.

Conversations on the Future of Scotland

These were the brainchild of Will Storrar, later Professor of Christian Ethics at Edinburgh University. Will had been coming to Carberry to write his book, *Scottish Identity* (published by Handsel Press): a chapter at a time, each weekend, which helped him conquer writer's block. He also produced a video to illustrate the book, which divided Scotland's cultural past into three episodes, the Medieval

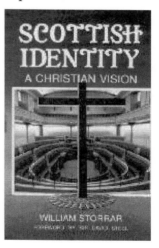

'Christian Vision', the Reformers' 'Godly Vision' and the Enlightenment 'Moral Vision' of Scotland. How we write history matters. As I see it, in all three periods, Scotland and England shared a similar vision, but the changes were sharper in Scotland, which Will illustrated very clearly in the video.

The cover of the book, to which David Steel wrote a foreword, shows the interior of the former Royal High School, then supposed to become the new Scottish Parliament building, and now possibly destined for a new St Mary's Music School.

Along with Ian Maxwell, who was completing his doctorate, we formed 'The Mair Institute'; John Mair – the other John Major – was a medieval philosopher who was professor in St Andrews and Paris at the same time. Under this hat we invited several leading politicians from all Parties to a good dinner followed by conversation. An example of the fruit of this was Donald Dewar meeting Alec Salmond and agreeing to campaign together for a Scottish Parliament – a meeting for which Will Storrar should receive credit.

Another was the change of heart and mind by Tom Nairn, author of the notorious view that Scotland would never be free "till the last minister had been strangled with the last copy of the Sunday Post". I remember an evening in the Beacon Room when he told me that he no longer believed that! Why did he change his mind? I think not so much because of argument but because of a level of trust built over shared meals and conversation.

After one specially controversial election result, with a clear majority of Scots not in support of a government voted in at Westminster, academics and arts people gathered at Carberry to form 'Common Cause', a citizen's forum for democracy. Inevitably I became the treasurer – as I have been the treasurer of a dozen and more organisations over the years.

These relationships were so important – they led to two 'Bus Parties', modelled on the efforts of Gunter Grass in Germany to include rural people in social and political discussion. For the first one I lent Willie McIlvanney a tie, and the group the Carberry minibus for the tour. It was, just, still the era when church and state could do things for one another without awkward questions being asked.

I wrote this poem on the second bus party, years later in 2014:

On the Runway

Crane fly challenging the breeze
alights, a tiny airship
on a paper runway. Six knees

genuflect upon a waiting clip
board, asking us to look
beyond a random insect trip

to what is stirring in the book
of Scotland's history, which we
are writing, questioning this fluke

of time which lets us see
so many possibilities, behind
September's serious apogee

of yes or no. I find
this fragile daddy longlegs
focuses the national mind

which flits between the dregs
of fear and sheer mis-selling
of the arguments. It begs

the issue, which is spelling
out in song and story who we are
and want to be: not telling

one another we'll be far
more wealthy if we choose
this way or that. The bar

must rise, so that we lose
our fatal lust for things
that rust and die, refuse

the lies, hold truth which brings
us hope, and trust that sees
our lift off come on gentle wings.

This second party of leading Scottish writers and folk musicians spent a week touring Scotland, performing and chatting with people about their hopes for a better Scotland in the context of the forthcoming Referendum.

We were strictly non-Party, which did not stop the BBC vetoing their initial plan to accompany the group, since they assumed we would be partisan. The poem was written at Stromness in Orkney, when a crane fly came and perched on my clip board.

Will Storrar, by this time director of the Centre of Theological Inquiry at Princeton, was the organiser. I had a very minor role as one of the bus drivers, but the great privilege was meeting and getting to know these committed people, including Neil Ascherson, David Francis and Mairi Campbell, Billy Kay, Hamish Moore, Karine Polwart, James Robertson, and renewing acquaintance with friends like Ricky Ross who joined us during the journey. One highlight was a visit to Freswick Castle, where Murray Watts entertained us to a meal and an informal ceilidh.

A Ministry to Rich and Poor

In Dundee I had felt that a city centre church, like a cathedral, must provide shelter, nurture and challenge for rich and poor. We continued this policy at Carberry, which meant offering a special rate to the unemployed, and allowing people from Urban Priority Areas to come and camp in the grounds. Ian and Elsie Moir were inspirational in their support for this.

> **Boundaries** *(Exodus 20.3-17)*
>
> *Look for the places without a boundary which might define them,*
> *the gentle earth, the open heart, the sparkling river,*
> *the light of heaven and the love-lit parts of earth,*
> *enjoy them, live with them and bless them.*
>
> *Look for the people without a boundary which might protect them,*
> *the poor, the sick, the lonely, those forgotten, strangers*
> *– no one should stop you also being there;*
> *desire those places and those people, give, receive.*
>
> *Because the law is there for bounded people and for bounded places,*
> *and it sets its own right boundaries,*
> *but in our weakness, law is not enough.*

Worship in chapel always came alive when Urban Priority folk were with us (as it did with church treasurers, strangely enough). It was not always easy; the rich do not always take kindly to rubbing shoulders with the poor; and vice versa. Carberry Tower was built for the wealthy, and as a hotel it has now reverted to being an upper class sort of place. However it was once traditional for the rich to patronise the arts, and we certainly tried to encourage artists and writers of various types to share their skills at Carberry.

To my shame I cannot ever remember encouraging poetry! At that stage my own interest was limited to emergencies; if I had to give a talk at the end of a meal, I would often seize a paper napkin and write a humorous poem, which was easier than trying to remember funny stories which I was poor at telling anyhow.

One day I had a visit from the convener of the Assembly Union and Readjustments Committee. He had come with some fatherly advice, "Jock, Carberry is going to close. You need to go and find yourself a big Edinburgh church while the going is good." Of course, the powers that be would have found it easier to close the place with me out of the way, just as it was only when Colin Day retired that Parish Education made their move to do the same thing. But I never took kindly to people telling me where I should go to feather my own nest, however kindly their motives.

I was already aware that the Church was battening down the hatches, and starting to sell off family silver. Anxious that we do our part, I had convened a meeting of all the staff, explained the Church's financial difficulties, and negotiated a plan that the lowest paid staff would take a 10% pay cut, and the highest paid 20%, in order to make sure Carberry was not loss-making. Proudly I took this proposal to the committee in Edinburgh. To my chagrin I was metaphorically booted out of the door and told I was doing a terrible thing, "We don't cut staff wages!" Margaret was with me at the meeting, and remembers that as we crossed George St afterwards, I said for the first time she could remember, "I am very angry!"

It seemed that the Establishment had decided that Carberry must close. However, by this time we had set up Friends of Carberry, and they included some people who got wind of what was afoot. Guy Douglas, John Mitchell and I met – Guy was a manager with what was then Hewlett Packard, and John was a Q.C.; we decided that the Friends of Carberry should bring a petition to the General Assembly. That would mean a proper debate, instead of the proposal being rushed through on the first morning under the report of the Assembly Council.

Parish Education were angry about our move, because they saw a second opportunity to get hold of funds from the sale of Carberry. I remember getting a formal letter one day, forbidding me getting any valuation done of the premises or repairs that might be needed (one of the arguments for the sale of Carberry was that it needed a new roof). It so happened that I did not open the mail that day until lunch time, by which time our surveyor had been up to look at the roof, and report that it was still good for many years!

Trusting the Roof

What is it about a roof that scares the horses,
or at least the sacred charioteers
who sit round tables at the head
of things. Roofs were built to last, and to outwit
not only those who steal the lead
but those who feel such cosmic fears
that stars might tremble in their courses.

When the Assembly met, we won the day. But it turned out something of a Pyrrhic victory, because the Friends were simply given permission to buy the house and estate from the Church of Scotland – even though it had been given free of charge by the Elphinstone family (after they failed to sell it), the Church argued that as a Charity they must get a fair price for it.

John Cairns, whose Dumbarton congregation was one of many who sent young people to Carberry, kindly agreed to help us in negotiations, and we did in fact raise the sum finally agreed as the sale price. But in my view that was money which should have been spent on upgrading the building. Looking back, I realise that I was politically naïve. When we went to Carberry, I later discovered, the Church had capital to spare, because of the sale of Christian Salvesen investments. What I should have done was say, "I will go to Carberry, but only if you give me £1 million to upgrade the building." I now know that back in 1986 I would have got it.

Ten years later things were different. I date the change from the time that our parent committee decided to centralise power, and (under the guise of saving money) insisted that even our light bulbs must be bought centrally. Of course, they had started to employ a member of staff responsible for all their buildings, and he had to have something to do . . . and in Scotland today I see the same thing, centralising of power and police, all under the guise of saving money. But then, it is well known what accountants say to certain company boards: "What would you like the accounts to show?"

After my mother died I grew a beard, which pleased Margaret, who became the family hairdresser. It certainly saved shaving, although by that time I had given up my father's old razor for an electric shaver.

Not Over the Top

Beards skipped a generation,
so my father's safety razor
was well used throughout the war
– that hairy war – to keep a major
trim, and smooth for each rough day.

One century later, I guarantee
this pocket survivor a sheltered life:
a short run up and down my neck,
just once a month, to please my wife,
not over the top of the chin (or a trench).

I lost two other family members round about this time. My half-brother Alan, who lived in Dornoch, and my half-sister Sheila, who was ten years older than myself, and died of brain cancer. Her own mother had died in childbirth, so my mother Da was the one who brought her up, and they always got on well. While as a boy I had enjoyed playing competitive games with Sheila, not least on the billiard table, I never had the chance to get to know her well, something I now miss.

Sheila

The sister that I never knew,
who dropped occasional gems
out of her crowded life,
as was her fashion, long
before I ever thought
such jewellery a passion
worth indulging. Of St Andrews,
where she failed to graduate
(pursuing hunting and romance
instead), she mentioned this:
"The minister saved my faith."

Hope Park Church, I think:
but who was he, and how was she
so thankfully delivered?

Something quite unexpected happened while we were at Carberry. The publisher managing Handsel Press borrowed from restricted funds to finance a book for Scottish Academic Press which never materialised, and was duly prohibited from running a company. I had to take the Carberry minibus at a day's notice and rush into town to collect Handsel Press books before they were impounded, and then found myself not only with the books in the garage but with a company to look after. The financial side was OK, but typesetting meant a steep learning curve; I ended up enjoying it, and even doing things like producing the international journal *Participatio* for the T.F. Torrance Fellowship as well as Kate's coffee table book *Mind's Eye*. As I write we have just launched a new series of Handsel Poetry Booklets.

To say the financial side was OK glosses over our change from being a fairly small Publisher to a very small one, and this was largely due to the International Theological Commentary. It was edited by George Knight, who had just retired from heading the Theological

College of the Pacific, and who was able to assemble a team of scholars from all over the world. The project was unique, but lost money for two reasons:

Its writers shared the neo-orthodox approach to Scripture which was fashionable in Tom Torrance's generation. But now it was too liberal for the conservatives, and too conservative for the liberals – a problem not unknown to politics as well as theology. With the exception of Walter Brueggemann's commentaries on the book of Jeremiah, and Bob Davidson's commentary on Psalms, the series did not sell well enough.

Eerdmans printed copies in U.S.A. and shipped us copies to sell from the U.K. That was a good model to launch the series, but neither of us spent the time and money on publicity that was required, especially because we were using lesser known writers from 'third world' countries, as they were known then.

Another thing I tackled was the rescue of the Scottish Church Theology Society. Founded in 1943, it had four objects, one of which was to apply theology to the understanding of issues of our times. I had not been involved for some time, but remembered it as a keen forum with a lively annual conference – but this conference was now attracting only just over 20 people, all older than I was. So I did a few obvious things like producing an attractive conference leaflet and talking to potential attenders; numbers went up to 60, and have generally remained between 40 and 50. Memorable recent speakers have included Tom McLeish, Janet Morley, Alex Salmond, Elaine Storkey, Stewart Sutherland, David Wilkinson and Tom Wright. One of the founder members, Ian Fraser, has just died; he was still attending in his 101st year, and I arranged for the Fraser Prize to be set up in his honour, now jointly funded by Theology in Scotland and the Scottish Church Theology Society.

Chapter Eight

SECOND INTERMISSION – HUNGARY

We stayed on at Carberry an extra four years, to enable its transition to an independent Charity – Lord Mackay of Clashfern graciously chaired the Carberry Trust, set up to allow all churches to participate in ownership. Dorothy Davidson continued as the indefatigable secretary of Friends of Carberry. This continued until some years after our departure, when a combination of difficult circumstances led to a merger with Gartmore, who ran a Centre in the West of Scotland. They took out a bank loan to upgrade the Centre, but that meant charging higher prices; the coming of a recession led to fresh financial difficulties, until in the end Carberry was sold to a hotel chain. More recently the building and estate has been in turn sold to Andrew Mitchell, who used to come to the Carberry Festival as a young man. The place is still run as a hotel, and popular for weddings.

It was important however for us to take our leave of Carberry, and we took time out to help us weather this huge change in our own circumstances, with the children now grown up. Time out in Hungary, staying in fact with one of our many volunteers from that country, Krisztina Nagy, who owned a flat in the Csepel district of Budapest, looking over the local cemetery (a very good view, compared to most urban flats). We arrived at Hallowe'en, when people thronged the cemetery and lit candles.

We were, of course, there to bury our own recent past and prepare to move on. People who lead intense lives at the head of Christian communities often need help with transition: perhaps this proximity to a cemetery, however accidental, would be just the thing! In Hungary people make long journeys to visit cemeteries, and flower shops do a roaring trade outside them. This was 1999.

The district was previously known as 'red Csepel' when it was a stronghold of Communist party and practice; but we had seen Hungary regain its freedom from foreign rule during previous visits. When our daughter started studying violin and piano in Budapest it was Communist, by the time she came back the regime had changed. Now we had come to live on this island in the middle of the Danube, downstream from the better known centre of Budapest.

Many older people were nostalgic for the years of communism, when everyone was guaranteed a job, and when – provided you joined the Party and kept your head down – you could expect some of the good things of life, like a Trabant car, if you waited long enough. The 'Trabi' was small, green, made of what felt like plasterboard, and of course there were stories of cars being nibbled by horses. We bought a second-hand Zastava, which was just one rung higher than a Trabi.

The politician Tom Mboya, sadly assassinated, served at a time when a Kenyan Government minister would send students anywhere in the world to get funding. He used to say that those who went to Moscow came back capitalists, and those who went to America came back communists! The grass is often greener on the other side of the fence.

One of the trees in our garden today is the *csaszárfa*, the Hungarian emperor tree (*paulownia tomentosa*), known in English as the foxglove tree . It has large exotic flowers, which really need hot summers and cold winters to appear, and we are still waiting for that. A member of staff in the Edinburgh Royal Botanic Garden told me that one was flowering in England – but as it was 30 years old he said we might have to wait a while. I wrote this poem for the Charity website 'My Time':

Foxglove Tree

Eight years ago I popped a seed
into a pot; that foxglove tree
is now three times the height of me,
and every year I yearn to see
it flower before I pop my clogs.

The Hungarian name must date back to the time when Hungary was part of the Austrian Empire. Few things from before have survived that long period of colonisation, followed in the 20th century by the

Communist occupation; one institution which has is the Kántus Choir in Debrecen, 'the Geneva of the East', a calvinist stronghold. I used to take the train across the country once a fortnight, and volunteer as an English teacher in the Reformed College there. There were, of course, a few emperor trees in the college courtyard.

In Debrecen

The other side of Tisza,
the tough side, the East side,
where the steppe is severe
and the discipline stark
stands the other Geneva,
supreme, strong fountain
of theology and science.

Orando et laborando,
college and church
are woven together
in a seamless vision
of Reformed life,
not forgetting meals
and music shared.

The Kántus Choir,
supple survivor
of Austrian rule,
Communist occupation,
sings high praise
to a surprised world,
soli Deo gloria.

The motto of the college was indeed *Orando et Laborando*, by praying and working, though nowadays a more rounded motto might be 'by praying, working and playing' – I recall teaching students Strip the Willow, which meant adding *bellekároly* (turn by the arm) to my knowledge of Hungarian. While I did spend two sessions every week learning the language – one with a doctor, the other with a teacher, each time spending an hour on Hungarian and an hour on English – I reckon that becoming for a short while a country dance instructor was the summit of my progress.

The Kántus Choir are world famous, and it is much to the credit of the college that it has continued to this day. I used to join them for rehearsals, and was so impressed that back in Scotland I was able to arrange two Scottish tours for the choir (who travel the world). They sing in German, English and Hungarian. Young people in Hungary want to learn English – when Communism fell all the Russian teachers retrained as English teachers – but older people often speak German as well as Hungarian, which reflects their past in the Austro-Hungarian Empire.

The architecture of parts of Budapest is modelled on Vienna, a day's boat trip up the Danube. Vienna is the home of the famous New Year Concert, which back home we enjoyed watching along with millions of others. However I did get fed up with it one year, and wrote my feelings into a poem.

The Dragonfly Polka

Vienna's annual claim to fame! A vast crowd cosies
up, and earns a New Year bonus for the camera crew.
Ban Ki Moon is in the gallery, with the eager noses
of some ninety nations pinned in adulation of a few
professionals playing on a stage . . .
                              A camera closes
on a glass dragonfly. All else is live, and polished too;
the dancers move – if choreographed to death – the roses
bloom on cue. On such a budget, we can view
the world, the universe! Or perhaps, in smaller doses
some old Austrian castles, high above the Danube – who
would grudge them status as museums? Who supposes
that this annual splurge is just a ritual, pew on pew
now stuffed with well-heeled worshippers? If a Moses
could appear, how would he cope with this? Do
you see him? Moses takes the stick from Jansens, poses
for the close-up, breaks the baton, hurls it through
the crowded hall . . .
                              and then the men in white coats
come; for this Vienna is not just the home of Strauss
you know; to meet religious nuts who burn their boats
is commonplace; to find your voice and lose your nous
is understood. The filing cabinets hold their share of notes
as well as concert halls . . .
                              We need to build a house
with humbler music, let the insects thrive
and keep the human race alive.

When we lived in Kenya, János Pásztor was teaching at Limuru. He returned to Hungary to become a professor of theology at Debrecen University, but it was the period when the church was under pressure to conform to Communist wishes, and in the end János resigned in protest at what he saw as corruption among senior clergy. Subsequently he relocated to Budapest, and became professor and dean in the Reformed Seminary there.

It was János who kindly arranged accommodation for our Dorothy when she went to study at the Liszt Junior School of Music, and it was János who arranged my visit to Pannonhalma to meet the Benedictine Abbot. The Pope had been to Hungary in 1996 to celebrate a millennium of Christianity in the nation. We had half an hour together, with Krisztina Nagy interpreting, and at one point I asked the Abbot, "You clearly have a position of great authority. Is there anyone to whom you are responsible?" The Abbot paused, smiled, and replied, "Well, I suppose I am responsible to the Pope – but you know, he only comes here once in a thousand years!"

Millennial Visit

Even an abbot has his fears:
sedition, plague, a nuclear war,
another Luther – or the years

may pass in Benedictine style,
well studied spirituality, rules
kept within a country mile,

each second silently ticks over
andantino, till the ruthless
papal calendar clicks over

and no abbot can resist it:
"A thousand years is just a day,"
he says, "it's past, and now you've missed it!"

The Pásztors had a family home in Szentendre, which their son Péter lived in after his parents moved to a small flat in Budapest. Péter worked as a writer and translator in Budapest. Some years later, one of his children tragically died in a road accident, and I wrote a poem for the parents.

The Accident

In memory of Domokos Pásztor, *váratlanul meghalt 5/8/12*

It came at night, sweeping
all our faith, our hope, before it;
left us numb, even our weeping

at a distance, out of our own choosing.
Shark-finned spikes of grief and dark
skinned debris trip our minds and memory:

tsunami-pinned, we cannot even park
our lives in sunlight for a second, never
walk a street without a coat of pain

which signals to the world to keep its distance.
Bare in private, bare in public, how can we regain
lost faith, lost hope, without the love of friends?

It was not always easy sharing a flat with a strong-minded person who had her own views. Krisztina and I fought like cat and dog for three months; every quarrel was, naturally, entirely her fault. However, after three months had passed, I began to ask myself, is it just possible that I am contributing to these continual fights? A good question. In the end I had to recognise that my upbringing as an only child, my military father and my boarding school outlook made me a very difficult person for some women to relate to. I have had to work on that insight.

I also remembered meeting a fellow minister, Ewen Nicoll, outside New College a few years earlier. I had greeted him perfunctorily. "What do you want?" he growled. I began to realise that I had grown a habit of 'using people' – with the best of intentions of course. These experiences, though hard, have helped me learn things which no doubt I should have learned as a young man. They have also encouraged me to grow my 'shadow side' – a piece of jargon which means that we can develop our hidden sides, enjoy doing different stuff, and doing stuff differently in later life, however unlikely that seems to start with. Poetry may be part of this.

Impossible Stuff (Isaiah 11.6-9)

Impossible dream, right enough:
just common utopian stuff?
Wee kids tending lion cubs?
Bears eating bugs and grubs?

Back up and focus on how,
consider the locus is now;
for Christians, the kingdom is near,
(outrageous) God's kingdom is here!

Take race and religion for starters,
why all these Middle East martyrs?
How well have you got your life balance,
the self and the shadow, for instance?

Peace making needs a first move,
however off piste it may prove,
so pray for key folk and their labour
and make sure you start with your neighbour.

An example of this 'shadow side' is how a person prays, and worships God. At one stage of life, words, and a good understanding, may be all important. But at another stage silence, candles, the arts, things like that can be very helpful. If only one person is leading worship all the time, the style may simply reflect their priorities and cut out others, so this is an argument for plural leadership in the church.

Six months in Hungary, with a short visit home at Christmas time, passed quickly enough, and thanks to that Zastava, we were able to visit many of the larger cities and towns in Hungary. I also had the chance to join a short 'mission trip' to the Ukraine with members of the Great Church in Debrecen. The main purpose of this day trip was to pass over funds and encouragement to one or two Reformed congregations in the Ukraine.

An eye-opener. The bus passed quickly through the border, thanks to a pre-arrangement that we would leave a gift of some paint. The economy was in ruins. We passed a deserted castle, which I was told was a kind of 'Potemkin Village' – occupied by local children twice a year who were rounded up to prove to the inspectors from Kiev that here was an orphanage which should get regular funding. (The inspectors possibly colluded in the deception – they knew how poor the region was.) A long day, spent in Western Ukraine which before the Treaty of Versailles in 1919 was part of 'Greater Hungary'. The present Hungary is about one third of that, deprived of the natural resources which were ceded to surrounding nations as punishment for being 'on the wrong side' of the war. That is the reason why there are still Hungarian minorities in the Ukraine, Romania and Croatia.

One of the many famous sons of Hungary is Zoltán Kodály. In Kecskemét we visited the Kodály Institute, now a graduate music school. His approach to music was more a vision than a method – he believed that every child should have a musical education 'starting nine months before the birth of the child' – or even 'before the birth of the mother'. Folk songs and the solfege method should be used to develop a well-trained ear, a well-trained intelligence, a well-trained heart, a well-trained hand, in that order. In Kecskemét Museum I also bartered my goose (bagpipe practise chanter and bag) for a zither; the director offered to get a set of Hungarian pipes made for me – for 50,000 forints, a reasonable price, but not one I could afford at the time!

My own pipes date from 2013, a lovely set made for the Grange Thistle Pipe Band. My teacher Jimmy Inglis was pipe-major of the Wallacestone Pipe Band, had acquired his pipes for £28 from his own mentor James Russell, a well-known player who lived at 'Southfield' in Larbert. When Jimmy offered to pass on his pipes to me, he insisted he would not take more than what he paid for them! So I bought his band some uniform, and now the pipes are insured for a hundred times that price.

Discerning readers will have realised by now that I am not only using suitable poems to illustrate the flow of my life, but allowing the text occasionally to flow in the direction of poems I would like to include. Having managed to insert two poems on porridge, here is one on bagpipes, or rather on one of the great classical pipe tunes, a pibroch which I am still trying to get off by heart.

MacCrimmon's Sweetheart

(a *piobaireachd* for the Great Highland Bagpipe)

In every family, a special one; and here
the F note lingers like a young man hoping
for a whispered word. The high A signals
his commitment to the peaks of love,
although so much lies hidden; in this tune
no double echoes heard, no testament
of whether she responded to his call.
We have the music: that is all.
Careful the courting, from urlar to crunluath,
strict form, ground and variations, with
a hint of passion in the taorluath doubling;
wave on wave of heart and head notes,
quavers cut and dotted, held on here and there
'as it was taught by Padruig Mor', perhaps,
and not in the academy: for the piper's art
(like romance) passes on from heart to heart.

The *urlar* is the ground, or base tune, of the *piobaireachd* (pronounced and spelt in English 'pibroch'), which is the classical music of the bagpipe. *Taorluath* and *crunluath* are the names of two particular variations, often played first as a 'singling' then as a 'doubling'. Padruig (Patrick) is pronounced 'Porig', and Padruig Mor means 'Big Patrick', who belonged to the MacCrimmon family who lived in Skye and were traditionally pipers to the MacLeods of Dunvegan.

In the interests of truth, however, I should confess that the name of a pibroch bears little relation to the tune itself. The original Gaelic name of this one, *Maol Donn*, probably refers to a cow that got stuck in a bog – not romantic at all. It's like how some African children are named – I remember one boy called *Nyama* after a piece of meat hanging up in the hut where he was born.

Anyhow, it was time to return to Scotland. There was an approach from Mayfield Church in Edinburgh while I was in Hungary, which I did not follow up, but the time had now come to find another job. It proved less easy than we expected, and by this time age was starting to be against us.

Chapter 9

CENTRAL SCOTLAND

We applied for a few churches without getting an interview. Nomination Committees often have a rather fixed view of the minister they want, and there were three things about us that did not fit:

We had been missionaries – dangerous, we might be 'enthusiasts'.

We had been out of the parish situation – even though we had transferable skills.

We wanted to work share – and although we had years before brought an Overture from Dundee Presbytery to the General Assembly on the theme of ministers work sharing, the practice was still novel.

So we agreed to do a locum in Kildrum Parish, Cumbernauld. The day we arrived was wet and cold. We had Krisztina Nagy with us, and when she saw the town centre – then at its crumbling bleakest – she commented "Ceaușescu's Romania had nothing on this!" Nevertheless we grew to love the place and its people, living beside the church in a manse which was something of a goldfish bowl. And we discovered a Stein family grave in Cumbernauld Village Cemetery (photo opposite).

There had been other possibilities for a man in his late fifties. The Scottish Bible Society was looking for a new chief executive, and I decided to apply. The application form was studiously non-ageist, but soon I got an embarrassed phone call: "We'd like to invite you to come for interview, but at the same time I wonder if you are aware of our policy that senior staff retire age 60?" So of course I pulled out!

The following year was 2001. Millennial fever had abated, but new forms of terrorism had appeared. The Lockerbie bombing was behind, 9/11 lay ahead. When I grew up, it was taken for granted that Christianity was normal – now we had to come to terms with other religions, and with the growing absence of religion in Scotland. There was also more study of religion as a social force, rather than a system of belief – indeed, a recognition that religion could be a force for good or evil.

Jihad

Jihad, scary word: yet beautiful to Nasser
and Reyaad, hating usury and vice
so celebrated daily in our media,
and ready to fight for something better.
Before we shake our heads, condemn
those militants out of hand, and
settle back into our Western ways,
let's ask ourselves whose fault it is
that those so quickly radicalised
have not been nourished in a deeper
jihad, rooted in the way of love,
not iron-fisted in religious glove.

We have had our own share of religious extremism, as the witch-hunts of the past showed, some even led by a past minister of our present parish church of St Mary's Haddington, back in the late 16th century. In those days St Mary's had a ruined nave, thanks to the siege of Haddington in 1548; a hundred years later Oliver Cromwell took an army into Scotland, and after some toing-and-froing either side of Haddington, defeated the Scots at Dunbar.

Oliver Cromwell

No 'royal calves' for this man's portrait.
Warts and all went onto canvas,
into lexicon, to glower at well-groomed males,
fash marketeers as he dashed cavaliers
who dabbed faulty potions on their faces.

'Nothing by halves' was Cromwell's motto.
Royal topping, Catholic cleansing,
selling Scottish prisoners into labour camps abroad:
dare-devilry, although he shared their faith,
ad-libbed similar notions in such cases.

Religious paths are free, he argued,
adding, "Get some Protestant skin cream,
or you'll foul the pores of politics, find my iron side."
Had Cromwell seen his butcher's wart, he might
have rubbed less caustic lotions on some troubled places.

Cromwell once practised cannon fire in one of the aisles in St Michael's, Linlithgow, a 'cathedral church' where I was once a member. We finally ended up joint ministers in a humbler church across the River Forth, in Kincardine, its full name Tulliallan and Kincardine,Parish Church, as there was a village of Tulliallan whose name is preserved in the Scottish Police College.

Unexpectedly it tied up with my family tree. The only minister on my mother's side of the family was a Simpson who had been minister in Tulliallan in the 18th century. On my father's side, there is an Andrew Stephen or Stein who lived in Clackmannanshire at the beginning of the 18th century; his eldest son John became a merchant at Kennet Pans, and his brother James farmed at Kilbagie.

Many farmers did a bit of distilling of grain on the side, and the Steins ended up running a distillery at Kilbagie. James Hogg, the Ettrick Shepherd, refers in one of his stories to 'Mr Stein, the distiller,'[1] and the story was written down by him in 1830. They sold poor quality hooch, I'm ashamed to say, until the Government in London imposed a tax which knocked out many of the producers late in the 19th century. The Steins intermarried with the Haig family and our name dropped out of the industry.

The Steins at one time also had a distillery at Kennet Pans. The only time I heard my father refer to this was in a slightly obscure couplet he used to recite whenever we passed nearby on our annual holiday drive up through Glen Devon to Boat of Garten: "Kennet Pan's an honest man, but 'haw haw' for Kilbagie." I think it referred to two farmers, or landowners, rather than the distillers, but it is true enough that Kilbaigie (earlier spelling) was the well known brand, as featured on my cousin Ian Stein's Mauchline Ware snuff box.

1 James Hogg, *The Devil I'm Sure*, Association for Scottish Literary Studies, Glasgow 2017, 68.

Kilbagie whisky was indeed famous, and the lines from Burns' poem 'The Jolly Beggars' go like this:

> And by *that stowp! my faith and houpe,*
>   *And by that dear Kilbaigie,*
> *If e'er ye want, or meet with scant,*
>   *May I ne'er weet my craigie.*

Kincardine is a small town which started off in Perthshire, migrated to Fife via Clackmannanshire, and remained in Fife, thanks to a local vote oiled by the promise of free bus passes in the Kingdom (as Fife is known). One of the Scottish physicians who attended the Russian Czars was born in Kincardine, and two centuries ago it was said that a whaling Captain from Kincardine used to go to Norway and talk in Scots to Norwegians, be understood, and vice versa.

I had by this time acquired the free bus pass that was offered throughout Scotland, and eventually wrote a series of 'bus poems' observing fellow travellers. Here is one of them – the title refers to the chariot belonging to one of them, which I used to see parked in the mandatory space now reserved for wheelchairs:

Liteway Number Three

Maroon, motionless, a phalanx
of metal tubes and craftsmanship,
lite in spelling, heavy in occupation.
Call him Harry, given that British flag
which signals provenance if not politics.

Smart, machine and rider, facing
back as bus demands, trousers
matched with top, stick placed
and tied as upright as its owner.

So far so much in common. Those
old soldiers press us backwards
into wartime, simple faith time,
here we go again time; reluctant,
our minds journey in reverse gear.

Unlike Harry. His gear is timeless,
flat cap contoured like the curves
around his face. A day is focused now
on simple things, like moving in and out
of buses, shopping, toilets, getting
home . . . and still: not breaking ranks.

As well as Tulliallan Police College, the Kincardine Bridge was in our parish. When the new bridge was 'pushed out' over the Forth from both sides, to join accurately in the middle, Margaret and I were invited as parish ministers to the official opening. When we arrived there were no name badges for us; we wondered whether we were meant to be there at all; then the receptionist suggested we should go through to the VIP section of the gathering, and there we were greeted with, "Welcome, we're glad to have you saying a prayer for the opening." The first we had heard of it, but as John Wesley said, "A minister should be ready to preach, pray or die at a moment's notice!"

I met Alex Salmond, saying, "Alex, you won't remember me, but you came to Carberry ten years ago."

"Indeed I remember", said the First Minister, "you prayed for me!"

There is a sequel. On the bridge were a number of disabled youngsters, including a member of our Bible Class. She was given an invitation to Alex Salmond's Christmas Party. Sadly she was by then too ill to attend, but on Christmas day there was a knock on her door, and the First Minister appeared bearing the gifts she would have received at the party. And I'm glad to report that he did not tell the Press, it was a very genuine act.

Under the Radar

The world is full of selfies, twitter feeds
and other acts of public gluttony.
Let's hear it for a well known face who leads
the way to do the decent thing, a litany
of private care; you'll know them by their deeds.

Tulliallan and Kincardine Church did not only have a Sunday School and Bible Class, it had a Boy's Brigade Company, and a brass band. The band had a persistent habit of coming first in national BB band competitions, which was a source of great pride to the company and to the village. I have always loved brass bands, even though I play in a pipe band myself.

Another musician turned up in Kincardine, Alec Shuttleworth, who came to us to complete his training as a probationer minister. Looking (and singing) a bit like Pavarotti, Alec turned out to be a fine preacher and great raconteur, who was to return to Kincardine as their parish minister a number of years later.

In the meantime, I had noticed a letter in Life and Work, complaining that no minister ever answered the questions the writer had. Being a sucker for this sort of challenge, I wrote in and was introduced to William Scott, who became a friend over the years. He had spent ten years exhaustively researching the site and scenario of the Battle of Bannockburn – getting original sources translated, crawling through bog on his belly, working through the physics of how the schiltrons operated, interviewing an elderly resident who could remember how the Pelstream flowed before it was culverted, and so on. I benefited from a personal tour of the battle site down on the Carse of Balquiderock.

Bannockburn

700 years ago they crept down through Balquhiderock wood,
in the early hours,
while the English slept off their carousing.
Out across the Carse
they marched, to park their pikes with Bruce
in front of Edward's camp.
The Earl of Gloucester saw the danger –
too late he charged
and fell. Ill omen
for the rebel foxhunt,
Scots too close,
the English cavalry and archers stymied.
Edward fled,
carried shock waves down to Berwick,
far beyond the Bannock Burn.

That is part of a longer poem called 'Shock and Awe', featuring the economist Milton Friedman as well as the Iraq War. At school I quarrelled with the history teacher, and have been trying to fill in the gaps ever since. William Scott helped, as did John Coutts who still runs the Poetry Group that meets in the Stirling Smith Museum. I wrote this poem for the friends of the Stirling Smith.

The Stirling Smith

So Scottish, so connected: the Smith hosts
samples of culture from Africa, America.
Museum, gallery and theatre, the Smith boasts
the oldest football, curling stone, memorabilia
of animals and Empire, heartlands and outposts.

Thomas Stuart Smith, from birth in Perthshire glen
was sent to school in France. He made the grade,
and took up tutoring; this Scottish émigré then
went off to Italy, to learn the artist's trade,
until Italian politicking sent him home. When

still Scottish, still connected, Uncle Alex
passed away intestate, nephew Thomas won
the legal fight for the estate, with economics
added to his arts portfolio . . . before he'd done,
the Stirling Smith was born, a charitable fix.

Cosmopolitan and gifted, Tom Smith passed
from Glassingall to Avignon in fifty something years;
painted 'The Pipe of Freedom' in his last
– offered to the Academy, rejected by their fears
of freedom, too much released too fast.

So Scottish, so connected: the Smith might
easily have matched the castle lift in Buda,
as the base for reaching to the height
with easy feet by way of a funicular;
tradition trumped technology in closet fight.

And now, the Stirling Smith's protected
by a faithful group of charitable Friends
who recognise that history's affected
by the gift of every person who intends
to make it still so Scottish, so connected.

The poem refers to a scheme to put in a funicular to take people up to the heights of Stirling Castle, which did not win the approval of councillors. The Smith Gallery and Museum is not funded by Stirling Council, and relies on public support. At the Museum I met Lesley Duncan, poetry editor for *The Herald*. She published the next poem.

Lonely Roads (Job 28)

Lonely the miner's path
Digging for gold, digging for coal
Digging for some victory?
More, digging for survival

Lonely the survivors walk
Children, brothers, sisters lost
Aleppo, Aberfan, the Iolaire
who adds up the human cost?

Lonely the philosopher
who lives uneasily inside us
seeking at every pithead
shafts of light to guide us

One sad event at Kincardine was the closure of Longannet coal mine. There were three mines, all linked. Mrs Thatcher had insisted one closed, which then flooded; the water found its way to the second mine, and then to the third, which was Longannet. So they all closed. Another chapter in the final saga of heavy industry in Scotland, which our family firm John G. Stein and Co. had been part of years before.

In Scotland, England and Wales, mining communities featured strong brass bands, and pipe bands. The Cockenzie and Port Seton British Legion band which I joined later on, had members formerly playing with those colliery pipe bands which no longer had a community base. At one point the stock of one of my drones split and I went to David 'Blue' MacMurchie in West Calder to get it repaired. Blue was an Australian who had made his way to Scotland, and his workshop was an experience.

The Piper's Cave

Here be no dragons, only a fiery
red bagpipe from Spain asprawl
a heap of junk, no longer breathing.

Aladdin's cave of stocks and ferrules,
parts and pipes from every Eurocorner,
brown newspaper cuttings, a wee thing

tashed, proudly pinned to celebrate
prizes now long past: bits and bobs
abound in black, no cauldrons seething

with a wicked brew, but here be Blue
himself with magic bags of competence,
enchanting players, that's the key thing.

Performers, politicians, and prophets are all seeking to 'enchant' an audience: to bring them under a spell, so they see things a certain way, perhaps so they do things a certain way also. With performers it is a temporary spell, though a lasting shift of perspective can happen This is the strong argument for funding the arts, though what comes back may clash with the spell which politicians seek to weave, always somewhere between a great vision and the immediate hope of election. Church ministers, who are called to prophesy, have deeper reasons to capture their audience, but also may be caught between that greater vision and the immediate needs of a church to survive. And challenging them all, that question "What is truth?" A question which defeated the Roman Governor Pilate, but is constantly before every kind of leader – as the prophet Nathan put it to King David in the Old Testament.

Up Close and Personal (2 Samuel 11 and 12)

Speaking truth
to power is always dangerous.

An aching tooth
must be removed by practised skill

not lightly tweaked
by wet-eared broadsheet journalists.

Nathan peaked
his art, and found the sharpest words

to wound the king
and send him firmly to his knees.

It was a thing
most cruel and wrong that David did

to Bathsheba
and worse, Uriah. Nathan's keenly

honed antenna
probed the festering palace gossip,

saw the sin,
and struck. Whenever someone high

to save their skin
advances crime, may prophets pounce.

I have mentioned my half-siblings, Alan and Sheila. The oldest in the family was Maisie, who had married an English solicitor and lived south of the border for most of her life. At this point she developed Alzheimer's, and went to live with her daughter Sheena in Blairgowrie. I used to visit her every few months and take her out for a drive. Initially we were still able to do a Scotsman crossword together. It was only after she had died that I discovered she had worked at Bletchley Park during the War - one of the remarkable 5,000 women who did so, many like my sister adhering to the 'sixty years of silence' rule.

Soon I would be retiring – at least for the second time, no doubt more work would appear. Once more I would have to consider 'the truth of my life'. On the religious level, I am a Christian by persuasion and to some extent I hope by practice, though the older I get the more I recognise my limitations. On the political level, an Anglo-Scot as I would define it in a neutral sense, and a Nationalist as I would define it in a non-exclusive sense, just recognising that to love someone you may need to do two different things: reach out to them, but also if necessary draw boundaries – the stuff of politics, the sorting out of politicians in every age. On the personal level, simply one human being trying to understand how to live well in a fast-changing age.

The Turner prize-winning artist Mark Wallinger had an exhibition in the Edinburgh Fruitmarket Gallery in 2017. As I gazed at his pictures of 'I', a serif shape of the capital letter, just like a steel beam, it brought back memories. The title of the poem refers to an adjacent installation, with lines of thread from a hall of empty chairs leading off into the distance, to a vanishing point Mark identified with the creation.

Vanishing Point

How can I vanish
when I am solid
as a steel I-beam?
It is my innocence
which rusts away,
ends my dream.

'Innocence' was another theme of his multi-faceted exhibition. I have always been captivated by the archetypal story of the Bible, how human innocence is lost and recovered through the journey of a single man who was called Jesus. A journey which is unique, yet which touches every person, every gender, every age, every place. A journey which embraced me.

I have not met many people whose conversion was as sudden as mine. Earlier in the book I gave a truncated version of a poem; the full version goes:

Changes

Let's style it black and white to colour,
that flash into an unforeseen dimension,
without drugs, dread, mania or magic;
just the unadorned power of what
a prisoner penned 2000 years ago:
"Behold, I stand at the door and knock;
if anyone listen, hear my voice, and open,
I will come in and share that life."

With such a pledged invasion of his privacy:
a child of post-war cleanliness could wash
the shit-soiled trousers of a snotty camper,
a son of lingering pre-war luxury
could let these prepossessions go,
decide not to preside at family board room tables, but to wait;
a youth brought up a Unionist become
a Scottish Nationalist for England's sake,
a man expected to embrace technology
find poetry more welcome to his mind and heart.

Such changes happen in unlikely places,
with all kinds of motives; and what better
reason for a teenager to rebel than when
a wiser friend comes in to stay, and say
"It's time to go another way; keep faith,
then you and I will work it out together".

'Friend' is not a bad word to describe
what later study would declare as 'Father,
Son and Holy Spirit'; God welcomes equally
the learned, and the simple, trusting child.

The extra verse above, not printed in italics, deals with the nitty-gritty of conversion – when God invades your privacy, asks you to do menial things, give up luxury, change your politics, become the new person God says you now are. All these are really the task of a lifetime, what Eugene Peterson called "a long obedience in the same direction".

I have had the privilege of meeting many committed people whose work made a real difference to the lives of others. Like Willie McPherson, director of the Vine Trust, whose main office is on a barge in the Prince of Wales Dock, Leith. He persuaded me to go to Peru to see the work being done among street children, and medical and dental services to those living on the Amazon River. Willie and others involved have sailed boats across the Atlantic so they could work on that river, and his record as a fund-raiser is amazing. His ability, for example, to persuade the Peruvian Government to support their work because it was being supported by Tony Blair, and to persuade Blair's Government to give support because the Peruvian Government was behind these projects, was awe-inspiring.

All this was long before Brexit. For an English nationalist, Brexit may seem an answer to prayer. For a Scottish nationalist, it seems like a mess; but climbing up out of mess has long described much of the human condition, and one of the marks of faith is the hope that God is rather good at that business (it's what resurrection is about). However, at this point in my life I was about to climb out of the driving seat in a particular Scottish parish, and it was nine years before the decision to exit from the European Union, still being worked through as I write.

I was still blessed with good health. At Carberry I had begun to hirple a lot, and when we got to Kincardine I went to the local surgery and was referred. The consultant said with a smile, "When someone is young and fit, we like to do two at once." What could one say after that? Thanks to the wonderful NHS and only three months wait, I got two new hips done in the main hospital in Kirkcaldy. Recovered from the operation, I was left thankful indeed.

Gratitude

Gratitude swirls through my veins,
hitching a ride on every corpuscle,
waving a fancy hat as it surfs its way
out of arteries, into capillaries,
a happy explorer sailing past
doubts and dangers, laughing at trolls,
patting monsters on the head, glad
to be alive, binoculars on the future.

Approaching retirement is not only about practical decisions: where to live, what things to dispose of, how a couple relearn the art of living together . . . It is also time for a hard look at what is going on in heart and soul. It is dangerous to be a spiritual leader! I think all ministers should have what is termed in the jargon a 'spiritual director', better perhaps just called a soul-friend. Someone with whom one can 'bare all'.

This idea came back to me when I visited Monet's Garden at Givenchy, near Paris. There happened to be an exhibition of paintings by Henri Charles Manguin, and in one painting (La Faunesse, Villa Demière, 1905) Jeanne, the artist's wife, is posed nude, with hands supporting on the ground as if ready for a race.

La Faunesse

To bare all, for the lover and the saint
opens God's gift, flashes the blocked colours,
soul and body naked before the one
who strokes, caresses with a hand or holy breath,
blesses what is offered with such patience,
free, poised for their eternal passion.

To bear all, for the artist and the saint
joins in God's work, grasps the unmarked lines
of soul and body till they cut the hand
that prays or paints them; colour flows like blood
presented to something, someone whose own hand
has signed each tree, each flower, each line of flesh.

To bare and bear all, for a God who puts
artistic judgment in the hand of a joiner,
unblocks every artist, writer, lover,
shines a band of light on leaf and thigh,
high on two lines deliberately crossed,
body and soul exposed in black and white.

It was at this time that I got involved with the Creative Arts Retreat Movement, known as CARM for short. Margaret for some years had been an art tutor and chaplain, serving one or two retreats a year at different English Centres. With retirement before us, I agreed to go with her to the Annual Consultation for tutors and chaplains at Swanwick. As we arrived, the retiring chair happened to be coming out of the door, greeted Margaret, then turned to me without being introduced and asked, "Are you an accountant?"

"No," I replied, feeling the finger of a recruiting sergeant pointing at me, "but I am treasurer of several organisations."

"We need you!" was the rejoinder. So I became their treasurer. A year or two later they realised I was also a minister, so I started to serve as a chaplain. One of the English Centres where I served was Scargill House, now 'resurrected' from sentence of closure by their Friends who not only raised money to buy it but provided the new Community to run it.

This coincided with the real death of Carberry Tower as a Christian Centre. I made a quick trip to the chapel to rescue a print which I had given to Carberry years earlier. More important, I took down to Scargill the lovely slate stone from the chapel, on which Liondsaidh Campbell had carved in Gaelic, *Ìosa Crìost*. She and her husband Angus-Peter Campbell had been part of the Carberry Festival. Years later their teenage daughter Brìghde, the first piper to study at St Mary's Music School in Edinburgh, would give a recital in Haddington St Mary's Church.

By this time I had retired for the second time.

Chapter 10

THIRD INTERMISSION – EAST, WEST, HAME'S BEST

A nice proverb – but where would home turn out to be now? People say that eighty is the new sixty. I still had a portfolio of interests, and was responsible for helping to run several Charities. That could be done living anywhere. But it was time to check out who I was, and where I was going.

Earlier I outlined *how* God had dramatically intervened in my life as a teenager. Equally important is *why* – and why *me*?

There are pragmatic answers which are more useful than speculating about the mysteries of providence. Clearly a shock was needed for a child brought up to wealth and power to become aware that 'the ground is level before the cross'. An experience like this certainly helped me to keep faith in an age when the West has been slipping further back into other ways of thinking. But in many ways it kickstarted change which would be healthy in anyone's life, however it happened. Over the course of my life I have been trying to learn:

- the importance of every human life, as well as the wonder of life itself

- how to develop self-confidence without falling into pride, and how to handle ambition

- the importance of beliefs and ways of governance which will protect the world and its people

- how the Bible sheds such light on Israel, church, earth and cosmos as well as on my own journey

The 'why me?' question takes us further into the mystery of God's will, and has been asked – sometimes in the form of 'why not me?' – by survivors of war and atrocity. It is a question which I think can only be answered by recognising that from now on your life must be lived in a special way, leaving other people better off and (if you are a believer) with an indication of the reality of God, whose love cannot be justified other than by saying his glory is revealed in the face of Jesus Christ.

I have never doubted the truth of Christian faith since my dramatic conversion. I used to get a bit fed up when I heard colleagues intoning how unless you know the reality of doubt you are not a true believer. And I got equally fed up with atheists intoning their litany of how the only truth someone can know is scientific truth, though I am trying to learn patience.

William Scott was largely responsible for this – a skilled mathematician as well as later on an authority on Bannockburn. We wrote long emails to each other. One idea which became clear to me may be obvious enough to others: a just God could never make it possible for clever people to believe just because they were clever, which is why no argument for God will ever on its own convince (even though believers can and should defend the faith – a practice which has the odd name of 'apologetics'). Paul even went so far as to say that the gospel was folly to Greeks (the intellectuals of the day).

Partly it is a matter of how we use words. David Hume did us all a favour by puncturing the pretence of bad religion. Here is what I wrote looking at his statue in Edinburgh's High St, at a time when Standard Life and Peveril Securities were heavily engaged in building work around St Andrew Square.

David Hume

His home swallowed by the makeover
of St Andrew Square, Davy Hume
has taken refuge on a High St plinth,
his wavy hair in green tinged bronze:
great excoriator of religious rot,
bare-chested, as befits a philosopher
determined to pare the apples
of conventional thought down
to the core, and spit the pips
at prejudice.
　　　　Upon his knee
he balances a stony reputation,
labelled by some wag "a good book
has no ending", flagging up
a dialogue still pending with more
than natural theology.

Since Hume, I think you have to be either agnostic or go for the real thing – you cannot simply look at the world, use your reason and say "there must be a god" (natural theology). Although the wonders of the universe have given many an atheist pause for thought.

Margaret and I both loved Edinburgh. By this time we had a small flat on the south side, and wondered about living in the city. I was actually born there, we had both studied in Edinburgh, we had friends there. And Edinburgh is of course a city of culture.

Book Festival

The old converse, the young have given
up their mobiles to the laughing gas
which rolls invisibly around the square,
perfumes every naked shelter pole,
finds a way to filter through the speech
of poets, journos, writers, politicians
– all this heavy chuntering of experts
needing air to light or lighten up
their flow of words, ignite a magic spiel
of intimacy, touching table talk
for those who like to make a meal
of meeting their celebrities. To feel
a breath of oxygen inflating lungs
long starved of air, that calms and cures
the chronic cough of technospeak.

Not that either of us are meeting celebrities, on television or in real life. It may happen occasionally – I once bumped into Sandy McCall Smith when he was leaving his house on the way to the airport, and he was as always courteous and friendly – but we are not celebrity junkies.

One of the lesser known attractions of Edinburgh is the annual Abbey Summer School. Founded by an American minister who worked in an Aberdeenshire parish, Matt Canlis, his theologian wife Julie, the biblical scholar Iain Provan, the writer Sharon Smith and others, it surfaces for a few days each year at Newhaven Parish Church. It always includes some kind of pilgrimage, whether to a place like Inchcolm or as a walk through the city. One year we went to Dryburgh Abbey.

Dryburgh Abbey

Seeking the mystery and ministry of stones
we sit in silence, carried by our expectations
through St Boswells, round and down to Dryburgh.
The whole earth is the Lord's – but here
the claim was staked with living stones
who entered the Novitiate Room, as we do now,
remembering their varied risks and reasons.
Pass to the Warming House, that single blaze
which fired their hands and hearts against the chill
of Border winters, climate little changed today.
Imagine the Refectory, meeting place for eating,
listening to the lectio, food for soul and body.

Build again the Cloister in your mind,
and take your annual book from off the shelf
to walk, reflect, absorb and maybe share
a quiet whisper with your priestly colleagues.
Down the steps they meet in Chapter, think of
white-robed canons firing comments and complaints,
working through the discipline of life together,
while the abbot rakes in all those living stakes,
God's croupier making risk a daily offering.
Above, they sleep on simple mats of straw,
and hurry down the stairs for nightly prayers,
their worship central to the abbey life.

Now the lights are empty and the walls are bare;
Historic Scotland shares a secular watch
with beeches, walnuts, hollowed punch trees,
Lebanon cedars, high limbs lost against the sky
in glorious puzzlement; young yews shoot
from ancient stumps, and we tread on surfaces
forgiving to our feet. No wonder Scott and Haig
chose Dryburgh as their final resting place,
for here the ruins hold their secret testimony,
that peace will win out over lust for war,
the pen is still more powerful than the sword,
and you and I are living letters from the Lord.

Our daughter Kate was married at Dryburgh Abbey, in the crypt which is through the centre doorway in the picture. There is still a poignant beauty about the famous ruins of Melrose, Jedburgh and Dryburgh, made a little more accessible by the opening of the Borders Railway, although nearly all visitors will come by car. I wrote a poem for the opening.

The Waverley

Once Innocent, horse powered
on the Scots gauge, hauling
deep-mined coal from Lothian pits
to bits of Edinburgh, falling
on a bigger stage, and British
gauge to lay me down to Hawick.
From where I was
to here, because
I run alongside history.

What goes around, soon comes
around; when Beeching's blades
cut rail, the people's protest
faltered, halted for a few decades,
but now the line's re-engineered
and cheered right down to Tweedbank.
From where I was
to here, because
I run afresh with destiny.

What is a railway? Who can say
where diesel-powered connecting rods
may drive our culture in its search
for access, links to all the gods
of steam or space we like to chase
when moving out of Edinburgh.
From where I was
to here, because
I run again, the Waverley.

Moving out of Edinburgh? We had not even decided to go there. We were still travelling, mentally. Knowing we had to put down some new roots, but also chasing after that elusive something we call fulfilment. It would be another year or two before I found that in writing poetry. But I always enjoyed trains. Some folk sit in coffee shops people watching. I do it on buses and trains.

Feed the Minds

The train commutes a billion bossy neurons
planning for the day, their owners sharpening
private worlds with coffee, crosswords, while
one empty page of middle age is noticing
that grizzled guy whose roving eye picks up
the flighty boredom of the glamour girls
behind me, whirls of hair and fashion,
chit-chat, layers of this and that.

We pass a shop front with a top front
message: 'Thinking Chocolate'. Possibly,
such double insight could indeed put right
the inner and the outer man, connect
the busy faces occupying places near me,
but a thousand miles away.

On that particular train journey I was heading west. Living now in 'the Far East' (Haddington) I think of the west of Scotland as 'the Wild West', though my own father went to school there (Allan Glen's). Margaret has cousins there. And Glasgow is also a city of culture – it's not all about deep fried mars bars – but different from Edinburgh, certainly.

Glasgow

City of Clyde, with strong well-founded banks,
city of patter, where they hunt wee jories
with a clothes-pole rammed down stanks;

city of culture, with Kelman, Connolly and Gray;
Glasgow smiles (and smells) much better
than does Edinburgh. There, they say

that Weegies laugh at jokes right out,
while Easterners nod wisely, wait
three days before they fall about.

City of Empire once, a rich man's club,
ashamed of poverty below the belt;
now reinvented as a trendy arts hub,

sugar packs so different from the sacks
imported by respected merchant barons
living well upon those black Jamaican backs;

Glasgow knows the way to kiss its enemies,
diss its friends, and keep its places green
for all the world, 'see you' a gruff disguise.

One Glaswegian we deeply admired – Geoff Shaw. His story was written up by Ron Ferguson in 1979, a year after Geoff died, having been a minister, member of the Gorbals Group and, famously, convener of Strathclyde Regional Council. He was tipped as a future First Minister, but (like John Mackintosh, who also died in 1978) his life was cut short.

In those days, Glasgow was solid Labour, with a deep sense of community which must have been rooted in a number of things, like:

- life in tenements with common stairs

- memories of war-time experience

- strong links with churches of all sorts

People were suspicious of Geoff Shaw until they really got to know him. Ministers were not supposed to be that involved in politics, but his track record of involvement with social issues, his home open to young people in trouble till all hours, his gift of friendship, won them over.

The following Brexit poem describes a scenario which seems light years away from the Scotland that Geoff knew, but funnily enough I had him in mind when I wrote it, a man as different from Donald Trump as it is possible to imagine.

Mufflers

I saw two men in mufflers walking towards winter:
Brexiteers no doubt, thinking Easter-tide
will soon be here, worth roughing it a little while.
Un-muffled winter, quite enough for most of us,
is when the gloves come off, and every safety net
we took for granted. Unforeseen, post-human stuff.

Today I fixed two woolen mufflers on my polytunnel.
They will save me two or three degrees of frost,
a temporary wrap, at little cost. Come spring,
they will revert to rafters, hibernate in summer.
What if global change produced another ice age?
Even hardened Scots might find that rather tough.

Across the Pond, they say even the cars wear mufflers,
embarrassed at emissions, possibly, or waiting
for the ace of Trumps to keep them morally
in play, no more downsizing. Mufflers silence all,
absorb the shocks which otherwise would open eyes
to recognise their emperors standing in the buff.

Glasgow was nominated the first European City of Culture in 1990. As I write, Brexit has just knocked Paisley out of contention for this title today. My own connections with Paisley are mediocre. My old Dundee friend Graeme Clark is now minister of Paisley Central Baptist Church; he is the designer of the cover of the new Handsel Press series of poetry booklets. And Paisley features in the following poem about the first victim of murder in the Bible:

Abel (Genesis 4:1-10)

Scots Version

Wha ur ye, Abel?
Colombian cottar, Feegie Pairk squatter?
Toon drap-oot, tuim flap-oot,
pastit or wastit bi Governm'nt cop oot?

Whar ur ye, Abel?
Hodden doon, trodden doon tae dust again?
Yer bluid is sae lief, it cries oot tae God
and tae a fowk makkit lyk im.

English Version

Who are you, Abel?
Colombian peasant, Fagie Park resident?
Urban drop out, hopeless flop out
pasted or wasted by Government cop-out?

Where are you, Abel?
Hounded and pounded into the dust again?
Your blood is so precious, it cries out to God
and to all the folk made in his image.

Ferguslie Park in Paisley, abbreviated in the poem, has been labelled 'the most deprived area in Scotland' – but I know some wonderful people who come from there. May Nicholson was one: she came off drink and drugs through a dramatic conversion, this 'wee wumman' who teamed up with the Duchess of Montrose and football legend Alex Ferguson to found the Preshal Mission in Govan (May died the year this was published). Cammy Mackenzie is another, minister of the Tron Kirk in Edinburgh. Ian Maxwell, who came to us at Carberry after being community minister in Ferguslie, is a third.

Appearances are deceptive. Here is another 'bus poem' overleaf.

Looks

He looked a hard man,
dressed in loose grey denim,
grey sleeves rolled up tidily
above his boxer's arms, lined
with faint furrows, like his brows,
face narrowed to that sandy red moustache
he wore, like stubble, with a grey panache.

He looked a hard man;
black rucsack colour matched
his boots, steel studded, starred
with squares of silver nail heads,
toes in pointed self-awareness.
The tiny pigtail signalled martial arts,
that chunky cheek scar came from Chinese darts.

He looked a hard man,
but his powerful hands
were buried in a black alsatian's fur.
The dog was whimpering delight,
gazing, rapt, into his master's eyes.
The looks that passed between the two of them
– with softer folk, there's precious few of them.

Buses are great places for unexpected meetings. Once I found myself sitting next to our local councillor, which was providential when shortly afterwards I needed his advice for a friend needing a council house, who had wrongly been labelled 'intentionally homeless'. By that time he was serving as Provost! Faith is always looking for God at work in things which others might label coincidence.

There are many fruits of Christian faith which have touched the life and culture of people who may not accept the beliefs of Christian faith. One is the view that all people are made 'in the image of God', so that every human being deserves respect and care: an idea which is being deeply tested during the current refugee crisis in Europe. The drowned child Aylan Kurdi is a symbol of this (his family like him called 'Alan' in English).

Refugee Status

The apples lie unburied in the grass;
one side is green, the other red,
but colours fade when you are dead
and lying at sea level.

The waves delivered Alan to the shore;
his skin was dark, and mine is light,
but colours fade when you take flight
and end up at sea level.

The Parties wait, uncertain in the main,
one brand is red, another blue,
but colours fade when you are through
with lying at sea level.

So pick the fruit, unblemished, while you can,
one side is red, another green,
but colours fade once you have seen
we're equal at sea level.

The people of West Scotland are great, and have a great legacy. But the West was not our scene. And our oldest daughter Dorothy, with her clutch of young children, might appreciate us being close. So we found a new home in Haddington, not realising at the time that so many Glasgow people post-war were re-settled in the town. Nor were we familiar with the story of St Mungo, whose mother (daughter of King Loth) fell in love with a shepherd, got pregnant and was cast out.

Mungo's Legacy

Not your usual jaunt from East to West,
to Glasgow or to sainthood.
Thrown by royal Loth off Traprain's cliffs,
cast adrift to cross the Forth,
storing up a trauma in the womb
to occupy a lifetime's therapy,
Mungo birthed at Culross, and the rest
is history – or legend if you will.

They came back, Mungo's bairns; re-settled
post-war streets in Haddington,
where they could nod to Traprain's bulk,
choose their own voyages of life and love,
without benefit of monks or ministers,
play leapfrog with the memory of Knox,
play catch up with the country folk
who know the score, and name each hill.

Here SNP and Labour vie to throw
each other's yoke off, fight or argue for
that Holyrood control, the saintliness
or ugliness of power – while Glasgow
maybe still remembers Mungo, with
his godly therapy, his special words
to calm the storm and cross divides,
his goodness spite could never kill.

We found a house, with the help of our son-in-law Francis, a chartered surveyor. He had just discovered pellet-fired boilers, so he built us a garage with one of these boilers in the back – as well as arranging to clear the overgrown garden and remove fourteen trailer-loads of debris.

Chapter 11

HADDINGTON AND COCKENZIE

East Lothian is probably an easy county for an Anglo-Scot to live in, in spite of the rivalry between SNP and Labour. referred to in the last poem. An English accent, which I largely have, is not going to exclude you from conversation or friendship. St Mary's Parish Church in Haddington gave us a great welcome, as is their wont with all newcomers. And I was happily accepted by the Cockenzie and Port Seton British Legion pipe band, although my background was very different from the other members.

How I joined was, I suppose, the fault of the Coop Funeral Society. By this time Margaret and I had agreed to do a locum at Cockenzie Old Parish Church. It so happened that the main local undertaker, the Coop, decided to invite all the ministers to a lunch. There I met the enthusiastic Robin Hill, minister of Longniddry. He insisted that I come to the Preston Lodge School Concert (Robin, himself a mean bluegrass afficionado and player, took a lot to do with the music at the school). When I turned up, I found myself between an attractive young woman and an older man; the latter, who had been an important local dignitary, was not best pleased when I failed to recognise him, so of course I began a conversation with the woman. She was Lynne Paton, a district nurse who also ran the pipe band along with her husband Rod, who was pipe-major. Lynne told me they had a large number of children learning to play. I was so impressed that I asked if they wanted any more adult pipers, and was recruited on the spot.

That was piping. I did also start doing a spot of drumming with the St Mary's Church band as a jembe player, possibly the easiest drum to play up to a certain standard – and they had an early service which I could go to before the 11am service in Cockenzie. I had learned to play the jembe in Kincardine, because it was simple to lead worship and play at the same time – easier than when you are playing a keyboard, for example. But that was earlier: in Cockenzie there was a fine young organist and keyboard player (who had his own band).

The Old Parish Church in Cockenzie has managed to resist all efforts to unite them with Chalmers Church in Port Seton, although they are close neighbours in a small town. They survive financially by letting their manse, and on the proceeds from their Gift Shop, as well as members' offerings. We were head-hunted by the session clerk, Angus Hare, and agreed to Sunday services plus two days a week.

By this time I was writing serious poetry. Here is one of my early offerings on that subject.

The Poem

Draw it down, work it up, serve it
hot and passionate like Andy Murray;
leave it cooling in a drawer, lonely,
vulnerable as any draft must be
to big events, to changes, fire, fatigue,
block, cross, clock, loss of energy.

Correction: this is me, waiting, kicking
heels against the wood, asking all my
urgent questions: "Top or bottom drawer,
open or shut, cabinet or tallboy,
town or country, nation, planet, galaxy . . .
where and when and who and how and why?'

Discernment: work in progress, facing choices
which will puncture poetry, or break out
the passion. Draw the hidden circles, call
your friends, turn a whisper to a shout,
for the drawer cannot sit as yours
to slide at will for ever; comes timeout.

'Work in progress' is a good phrase; "a poem is never finished, only abandoned", is a well-known saying. Retirement itself was a work in progress, and it would be five years before we retired for the third time. Meantime there was a large garden to re-build . . . it took me three goes before the lawn was presentable, and flat enough for a game of crocquet.

Traditionally, employment in East Lothian was in fishing, farming, or mining for coal. One of the mines was called Parrotshot, and gave rise to a street name I saw on the bus going into Edinburgh. I wrote this poem before I knew the origin of the name.

Parrotshot

Who got to name this new suburban street?
An ageing Monty Python fan? Dead parrots
do not form a queue before the mortuary
in eco-friendly towns like Edinburgh.

More likely, some raw parrot keeper
found his pet in season, lashing out
with tongue and beak and claw
(as parrots do when naturally
warming to the other sex), or
even bowing to his owner
as potentially a mate.
This keeper did each
week the Scotsman
crossword, aided by
his pet's vocabulary
(its angry language),
till the flyting turned
to biting, the necking
changed to pecking,
so that 'parrot's hot'
inflamed this man to
make it 'parrot shot'.

A big issue in Cockenzie was the closure of the Power Station. It was already a shadow of its former self, with much of the work being done by contractors instead of local people employed directly by Scottish Power. Before it was built, they had worked in the mines. But it was about to close completely, which led to a fractious three-cornered debate between the owners, East Lothian Council, and a local action group, which is taking years to resolve. The third section of the poem below reflects that debate.

The first bit of demolition was the chimneys, followed over a year or two by the main station, which towards the end looked from a distance like four dogs sitting in a row. The chimneys had been a key landmark, as I could see when Archie Johnston took me out in his boat fishing for lobsters. Archie was a key figure, with his feathered bonnet, leading the 200th anniversary celebration of the Fishermen's Box Meeting; 'the box', which has a double lock for two key-holders, used to hold the cash collected to support fishing families in need; it was ceremoniously pulled out from under the table in our vestry, where it had been lodged.

Cockenzie Power Station

1 Farewell to the Lums o' Cockenny

Grey and white across the sky
fly shrouds and cirrus clouds;
above the Firth, the Fife hills flit
from west to east, and brush
a laid back, painterly horizon;
shore lines match this movement,
picture framing work and living space.

The vertical begins far down, where
hidden shafts lift coal from underground
to make a profit out of power.
Two chimney stacks take over, bound
up and away, cock a Cockenzie snook
at flat earth thinking, lift our hearts,
change landmarks to blue sky marks.

Sailors set their homeward way by them,
golfers guide their forward play by them ,
locals spend their every day by them –
but not for long. Already, pylons hang
their empty cables in a sad catenary,
without a whimper, let alone a bang.
The universe tomorrow's horizontal.

2 Waiting for the End

Four ghostly hoppers face the concrete
music of demolition, sitting upright,
aghast, like dogs on death row, linked
by frozen metal leads, sad skeleton
of Scottish Power.

No, this is not a post-referendum poem,
just a header through the empty space,
without the chimneys for two goal posts.
A ball of words could skiff half o'er
to Aberdour,

and sink the workplace memories
respectfully within the Firth of Forth.
Soon the levelled landscape will
shrug off its past, and host an outcome
sweet or sour.

3 Boxing Day 2015

This empty box has folded – its time and space
exploded, christmas past, new year no' here
yet. Yet what?

Exit stage left, braw bygone social age,
your rage expired with Scargill and McGahey.
Wait. For what?

We live on private festival left overs,
meat digested, leaving us in flesh and
bone somewhat

confused, dry, knowing that the feast
has left a debt, but how can we afford
to run what

ought to be a welfare state, now saddled,
bridled with demolishing austerity, to
pull down what

we built with hope, a level playing field
of health and education for a kinder world.
So, now what?

Gap site, dusted down, for someone fly
enough to seize the day and fly a kite
to save what

should be our own foreshore, not the private
land of strange investors? Who and how and
why and what

are public questions. After Boxing Day
the local people want their say.

Port Seton was famous as the childhood home of the painter John Bellany. His friend Alistair Hamilton still runs the Harbour Gallery, and we were given one of Alistair's paintings when we left Port Seton.

Scotland is something of a village, and it was the young student mentioned in chapter six, now Dr Janet West, who phoned me when John Bellany died, saying, "I'm his G.P. The family are wondering about funeral arrangements, can you advise?" It so happens that Margaret was at Art College with John's first wife Helen (also his third wife – they remarried). Of course, in the end, John Bellany got a grand send-off in Edinburgh St Giles.

John Bellany

He painted women, men
and fish, boned big scale,
painted them into his life.

He painted place, Eyemouth,
Port Seton, harbour and coast,
held them fierce and tight.

He painted all night, white-hot
with art, drink, passion, while
his family tried to find him.

He painted to blot out the pain
as that new liver struggled with
its flitting to an artist's body.

He painted the light, the music
of Tuscany, that Indian summer
when the ghosts were laid.

His son Paul filmed and produced a documentary for the BBC on what it was like for the family living with an alcoholic who finally got a new liver. He kindly gave us a copy which we use on CARM Retreats because it is full of Bellany paintings as backdrops for the scenes.

After five years we retired for the third time and focused on life in Haddington, with Sundays playing in that church band. I don't really approve of bands which don't meet for rehearsal, but the other players were all so competent they didn't need to, and I shelter happily under their umbrella.

St Mary's is 'the town church'. There must be very few congregations in Britain where the local MSP will serve you bread at communion, and the provost of the town serve you the wine – as happened to us, from two men with servant hearts for church and community.

The Common Cup (Psalm 116)

At the September 2018 Communion in St Mary's, Haddington, duty elders included Iain Gray MSP and Councillor John McMillan

Iain finds us bread, the kind of thing
an MSP is voted in to do,
while John behind gives out the wine, he too
enriching public service, entering
our temple courts as one of us, like when
the link of church and state was sacrosanct,
and here the Provost of a Council ranked
no higher than the least of other men
and women. Clasping hands around the cup,
we drink a portion rooted in a psalm
which pulls us back to Passover, then rolls
us on through three millennia, wraps us up
within the love of God, whose pouring arm
can ground and heal and feed all souls.

The building itself is remarkable. The 'rough wooing' of Henry VIII knocked half of the church down, after which John Knox got a wall built in the middle, the rest lying open to the elements for four centuries, but in the 1970s it was restored and the whole building is now well used, with services, exhibitions and so on; it really functions as a modern cathedral should.

I was surprised to discover that around 1640, a century after the Siege of Haddington, when Cromwell was in the ascendant, the citizens had forgiven the English to the degree that "the borough of Haddington declared their consent to be incorporated into a Commonwealth with England";[1] this was well before the Union of Parliaments, and perhaps reflects the religious bond many Scots felt with the free-thinking Cromwell.

In 2013 I joined a workshop on Celtic spirituality in St Mary's, and wrote this poem.

1 W.F. Gray, *A Short History of Haddington*, SPA Books 1944, 44.

Pillars

High, high reach these pillars in their praise,
shouldering the arch which spans the space
you occupy, our God, with silent shoulders
holding up creation, as a cross once held
you pilloried: such an unimperial way
to fix the fallen architecture of our race.

Hailes Castle is a ruin not far from Haddington. One day I took the bus to East Linton and walked back to Haddington along the River Tyne. I had a fine view of the Castle, though I had to visit it another day to find out its connection with the Earl of Bothwell who married Mary Queen of Scots.

Hailes Castle

Eight centuries of rest and ruin,
with the blind river seeing all
and flowing over every folly.

Near the castle, ivy is abseiling
down a cliff below the blossom
spreading white under a blue sky.

A wren scolds; wild garlic unfolds
its annual perfume which young
Jamie Hepburn must have smelt

while splashing in the Tyne,
before his tumultuous affair
with Mary Queen of Scots.

Ivy cloaks the generations, but
if we tear it back too much,
what will we find?

After the 'tearing back' in our own garden before we moved in, we found that the beech hedge at the end of the garden had become too thin and straggly to make a screen. So it too was pulled out, and replaced by a wall. Then we found that our sitting room had a green curtain outside the window, and we decided to cut the fuchsia outside right back. But a year later, the curtain was back again!

Fuchsia Magellanica

She came knocking at our window
the summer after we arrived,
like a neighbour
reluctant to intrude too soon.
We turned her away, cut her dead
– or so we thought.
She did not take offence,
but waited, politely, for a year,
out of eyesight.

And then, one quiet afternoon
I saw cascades of lady's eardrops,
sunlit rain forest,
jewels worn for the first time.
Now she makes an annual visit,
dressed in purple,
stays a few months, causes no trouble,
eyes downcast, but ears well stretched
for our applause.

Amber also was waiting for us. She belonged to a neighbour, and visited our garden regularly for several years. One day we left the door open, so she went in to case the joint. She liked what she saw, and became a regular visitor. Margaret fed her . . . and in the end, she lived with us – till she died in her 22nd year. I wrote three poems about her, at intervals.

A Circle of Comfort

A circle of comfort, inclusive
tail wrapped into the circumference
and gently laid on two hind paws,
pushed a little proud
to pillow a head in dead sleep.
One old ear stays open to the world,
another paw covers the mouth,
for cats have much to teach us.

Ageing Paws

She walks slowly now, seeing
just the object of her need,
no longer good at listening.
She would vote for anyone
who pledges food and cuddles,
shares the sense of where she's at.

She sits, exuding memories
in the gentle sheen of her fur,
a chancer clinging to one extra year,
no word about death, or matters
save those softly screeched complaints
about arthritic joints, and this and that.

She perches still atop the desk,
ignoring files, coffee, paper clips,
no qualms at stepping on a keyboard,
ignoring key strokes of philosophy
in favour of immediate needs –
some chicken liver, and a pat.

She lies, a solemn silent witness
to our history, and soon to carry
past and present to a garden grave.
We shall bury her with quiet grief,
just as she is, her unique legacy
those twenty years of being cat.

She holds up to the moonlight
all our fraught catastrophes,
captured in four ageing paws
which cling and creep, and scratch and sleep:
a balanced life, never controlled
on anyone's computer mouse mat.

Farewell Amber

I watched myself pouring soil
with love upon the chilled fur,
tears forming fresh like dew
as the cold earth covered her.
A stone, small like the size of cat,
rests beside her grave: a friend
she was, strong-willed, affectionate,
her own catself right to the end.

Chapter 12

AND NOW?

It is the year end. Time to look back, and forward. To keep my mind active, I have started a PhD at Glasgow University, in the area of theology and creative arts, with two fine supervisors, Doug Gay (principal of Trinity College) and Alan Riach (professor of Scottish Literature). The idea came to me from Fiona Rew, a Glasgow community worker attending the 2017 Wayfarer Arts Conference at Lee Abbey, where I was leading a poetry workshop. I suppose this is one of the bigger boats I have pushed out in life, and I hope I can still row.

Year End

So ends this year. A vine and diary trimmed
to short endeavours – one to focus energy
on coming fruit, the other into blocks,
tired lengths of tinsel draped round winter days
which carry on as every year before them.
What thing will bring my diary back to life,
to bud and fruit with new-born godly purpose?
Weekly tasks resumed? Engagements unforeseen?
Intentions written large on empty weeks,
no doubt to find themselves cut down to size
and stuffed into a vacant day or two?
No, Spring! In nature and in every thing.

I found some inspiration in the border next to our beech tree in the centre of the garden. One lupin insisted on flowering all the way through from October to December. Such a brave flower deserved a poem.

Rebel

Bold choice, to flower in winter,
contradict the book
and cock a coloured snook
at what's aye been the norm.

Lupins should retire,
drop seed, and go to ground;
a few leaves stay around,
but not above their station.

Strange gardens, stranger times
provoking summer plants
to climb the seasons, chance
the cold, hold up a flag.

How and when lives flourish is one of the themes of spirituality. For many years Margaret and I have gone to (different) 'spiritual directors' as they are quaintly called – 'soul-friend' is perhaps a better word, except that there is a form of professional training in Ignatian spirituality which directors undergo (and which Margaret and I did while we were at Carberry Tower).

I have had three excellent directors, two of whom have died. The first was Archie Mills, a sailor who became a Christian when he read the story of Paul's shipwreck in Acts, as he felt the description of the storm was so authentic; subsequently he became a Church of Scotland minister, then worked in the field of personal and corporate development; he was also on the Carberry Council. The second was Michael Butler-Burns, once a Roman Catholic parish priest in Edinburgh, but over the time I knew him, he moved into full time work as a trainer and consultant.

In Haddington we have become part of the Lantern Group, consisting of folk trained in the Ignatian tradition. It meets monthly, and two or three times a year runs a Quiet Morning for others to attend. This has settled into three usual places, Coldingham Priority, Holy Trinity Church in Haddington, and Ormiston Parish Church. In the summer the group have a day retreat somewhere. One year we met at a house called Beech Hill; Andrea DePree had made a wonderful garden, and beside the house she had parked three boots with flowers growing out of them.

On a Retreat at Beech Hill

Three old boots –
tongues hanging out
marked 'outdoor adventure' –
tired of tramping farms and fields
relax on the garden steps
and open their uppers to pansies,
saxifrage, nemesia: proof
there is a world above their soles,
a world of blue and purple, purposeful
and peradventure come to flower
most gloriously
in later years.

In my case it is poetry that has come to flower, and I enjoy being part of Tyne and Esk Writers, which has nine groups meeting throughout East and Mid Lothian, each group with a mixture of experienced and new writers. Two of the groups are specifically for poets, the other groups are mixed, and they all provide fellowship and encouragement as well as practical help with good writing. In my time we have had a wonderful succession of Creative Writing Fellows: Tom Murray, Claire Askew, Catherine Simpson, Russell Jones, and now Margaret Skea.

In Margaret's case it is using her art training to work with individuals and groups, and often to provide a centrepiece for small gatherings. Currently she and another leader lead a WAG (wee art group) twice a month.

After a meeting of people from Haddington West Church in church premises at East Linton, I wrote this, reflecting on what Margaret was doing to take people into an experience of meeting the risen Christ beside Lake Galilee.

The Lord's Breakfast (John 21:1-13)

She builds a fire with beach sticks,
sets it alight on the lounge carpet
with a bright red cloth, beyond
the pebbled scattering of sand,
the waving blue gossamer sea
jumping with tiny glass fish
eager for a share of the action.

She tells a story of seven men,
lost at losing their best friend.
How they spent an empty night
on an inland sea, fishing memories
from their own internal Galilees.
Sunrise, and a voice inviting them
to make their failure public news.

She brings to life the eighth man,
drawing fish and fishermen together
to identify himself, and tell them
it was breakfast time. She sings
a grace song, breaks a loaf of bread,
shares a meal that lets the fish man
weave the carpet of our lives.

One unexpected piece of writing was due to a long past relationship. John Clark is a retired dental consultant in Dundee. He began to make friends between the Steeple Church and the Muslim community in the city – it was in fact out of this that I was invited earlier to write the poem 'Back to the City' for a city festival (chapter 6). Now he found that two Muslim academics were asking for dialogue on the subject of charging interest, something which Islamic banks do not do (or, some would say, manage to find ways of getting round). The upshot was that the Steeple Church minister asked me to meet with them.

We had an initial meeting which involved groups like 'Positive Money' and 'Rethinking Economics' also. Then they asked if I would contribute to a joint paper for a business journal, with an initial talk at a symposium at Napier University. Later I was asked to contribute a poem for a conference on the world's largest infrastructure project, the Chinese 'Belt and Road Initiative.

Belt and Road

Like a good poem, this initiative has form:
each emperor, each president a legacy.
Why not? The world is starved of big ideas,
longs to open technological silos, feel
the flurry of capital flow, slip a snap-ring
on the belt of progress, label fears
of failure just so many Chinese whispers.
Who wouldn't rush to buy a bigger suit
instead of tightening belts through barren years?

Remember Truman wanting closure, hating
those two handed economic pundits
juggling upsides, downsides which would keep
the options open, safer since rough
politics will trump their models, stuff
the plans of presidents; that great leap
forward might confuse the Tao somewhere,
bold infrastructure bear the tracks of tanks,
not trade, or nations drift back into sleep.

One road, one belt: to keep economies turning,
wages paid, Tajikistan lights on,
the Silk Road born again for industry
and culture. Not a solo but a chorus,
so they say, a symphony of many players,
with no mention of conductor's fee;
for music on this scale we need a key:
the martial black belt, with such heavenly colour
– or, the broken-belted bumble bee?

Muslims and Christians both think about fate, though in rather different ways. Cue the dialogue between fate and freedom, introduced in chapter one. When the theologian T. F. Torrance was an army chaplain, in one battle the soldiers on either side of him were killed, but he was untouched. That experience drove him through the rest of his life with a deep sense of gratitude, and sense of calling. But what about those who suddenly fall, like the cyclist Pat Kenny, knocked down by a car?

Questions

i.m. Pat Kenny, died 21 Jan. 2011

What drives a man with rotary feet
that push past road race records,
jump from bike to tandem trike,
towards their target of a million miles?

What drives the spinning wheel of fate
to knock this wonder off the road
of life, in one split second smash
– age 72, and ninety thousand short?

What drives the rest of us, whose fight
for fitness ends up fitfully, to speed
through town and country in our cars
so someone else may join the stars too soon?

What drives a lonely figure, fraught
with faith, philosophy and more,
aka prophet, son of man, etc
to say: 'First last, last first?'

And if we are driven, as I would admit is the case with me, where does that come from? Our head, our heart, our gut? Can you read character off palms (or tea leaves, or anything else)?

Lines

This life line creeps across my palm,
then hesitates, unsure. So maybe
I should keep my palm unclenched,
no sense in tempting providence.

The heart line on my other palm
is knocked away by head line; it
was always thus; the space between
has caused a scene throughout my life.

Clasp my hands, then heart and head
go skin to skin and make their peace
with life – a touching thing, no doubt,
but is that folding prayer, or sleep?

Here is another poem which reflects on the idea of fate, thinking of the book of Esther in the Old Testament.

The Mills of God

We see them going through the mill,
victims of crime
or maybe just someone's ill will;

how commonly God loses teeth;
time after time
those mills take us beyond belief

into a world where fate just leers
and borrows names
like Xerxes, surfacing the fears

of Jews, who fear that they will die
through vile games
by Haman, foe of Mordecai.

No righteous Miller's mentioned here,
no gumsy God
is slagged for failing to appear,

but Esther's faith and courage show
how all in all
the mills of God grind slow,
but grind exceeding small.

One of the interesting questions which get asked when people want to 'get you talking' is whether a person, left to themselves, lives in the past, the present, or the future. When I was at school I certainly lived in the future, often worrying how I was going to cope when the next big thing happened (becoming a prefect, taking an exam, leaving school, whatever). I have had to learn the meaning of that Latin tag *solvitur ambulando*, that things work out as you go along.

I once had doubts about 'ambition', thinking that a devout Christian should just let everything come to him or her as part of God's providence. I have changed my mind; to have ambition is part of our humanity, although it is not always easy to distinguish properly our ambition for ourselves, for others and for God – and sometimes, difficult to work out what our ambition for ourselves is, or should be.

Ambition

Braeriach topped, high boast
for the lad knowing little
of adolescent horizons, but
foraging post-war climates,
climbing childhood as he
climbed that cedar,
creating a carefree cave,
high above the crossfire
of home and school.

Ben Cleuch barefoot, shoeless
(but not like father as a boy);
drumming to a different beat,
dumping hard-won inheritance,
ditching horses and high living
for the low life God spelt,
sounded, flashed before him
like the call of the Cairngorms.
Mountains out of flattened earth.

Upper Circle, Usher Hall:
Menuhin plays Mendelssohn,
and every bar and beat
of teenage surliness goes
spiritual, a spaceship
surfing unknown galaxies
and coming home, still
innocent of love, though with
a tendency to overdrive.

Jump sixty years, a flash
of time. Purse your lips, and
parse your shortening life,
the love you've found.
That emperor-tree, how
long until it flowers?
This new career in poetry,
a seed in unknown soil:
A cave? A mountain? Outer space?

Travelling home on a train through the north of England I wrote three linked sonnets, with the same questions about the future, still marvelling at how fate and freedom run rings round each other.

Towards Sundown

Sunset sorties behind a ragged cloud,
sky somewhere west, Northumberland.
Puffs hang heavy, pause to catch some breath
before they regroup, tease the dying light
and work out fresh their boneless grey anatomy.
These fading clouds of circumstance cheat death,
negotiate with wind and rain, while we
suppose the universe is black and white.
A turbined windmill turns a trefoil blade
in languid triple time, a casual tribute
by the engineer to trinity. Beyond
the sweep of Lindisfarne, a balustrade
of fog guards access to the east horizon
while the experienced Virgin train flies on.

A tractor working late now pulls a square of red
along burnt umber furrows. One beech skeleton
waves aloft its rotting, whitening limbs
at any passenger who lifts an eye, takes in
their rooted residue, gazes further on
to where the sea gleams, as the daylight dims
over the fields now green with the sheen of Spring
and such relief, as flood gives up its pin-
hold on the ground, and surface water dies.
Seagulls hang upon the breeze, a tanker
shines in silver line, the light and dark
play open air Othello, add surprise
to evening's steady programme of decline,
this fateful daily haemorrhage of sunshine.

The train past Berwick curves this way and that
and makes the setting sun play hide and seek
up to the edge of Torness square and squat,
but full of energy upon our seaward side.
A lighthouse stands without a light, perhaps
with buried memories of Eyemouth, what
it saw that night of doom. The Lomond Hills
stand out to mark the land and sky; beside
the shore Inchkeith lies low; while Arthur's Seat
remembers congruence of church and state
where king and anchoress shared public trust,
when faith and chivalry spurned counterfeit.
Gone is the wind, the sea, the mist, the sun,
what shapes our future, when the day is done?

There is a vulnerability about human life, which calls for compassion – not least when a person believes in a God who embraced our vulnerability inside Mary's womb. I have been privileged not yet to slow down as much as many of my age, but I accept that it will come. Till then, like Sam Will, I will head for the tape.

Living on a Concertina

I am lurking somewhere vulnerable,
between the squeeze and the spread,
dodging the music that would pin me
to a single note, yet filled with a dread
of everything hung out, seen and heard
at full volume, trumpeted, exposed
to the scorn of every casual listener
– or shut away for good, silent, dosed
with valium at the graveyard end
of the performance. No, let me
tread that middle way, balanced
a capella on the box's edge; set me
somewhere grazioso, con amore,
for I must find the words to write
before I sense that rallentando
which will take me into night, and light.

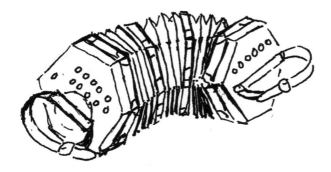

Like a concertina, we breathe in, we breathe out. That breath sustains us for the outer journey, and for the inner journey. It is all the gift of God.

Postscript

MY VOICE

During research at Glasgow University, I was asked to write a paper on 'My Voice as a Poet'. Here is a shorter and less formal version of that, followed by reflection on 'My Voice as a Christian'.

I started writing serious poetry ten years ago when I was nearly 70, mostly on politics, economics, nature and modern life. Five years ago I felt a call to write on Bible themes, and have published a book of poems on the first six books of the Bible. I realised that writing 'poetry on poetry' – as with the Psalms – would be different and difficult, and so took the opportunity of the new PhD offered by Glasgow University which incorporates creative practice.

Poetry is about making connections, sometimes unusual ones, and in my poetry (and life generally) I try to find and make bridges between areas of life and thought that are often kept separate, for example:

- Faith, politics and economics
- Religion and spirituality
- Traditional and contemporary
- 'Conservative' and 'liberal'
- Transcendent and immanent

There are many types of poems. Two of the main categories are lyric poetry and epic poetry, but I don't think I write either, though I admire them. If it didn't sound pretentious, I would go for the label 'prophetic poetry', at least some of the time. 'Poetry of enquiry' is perhaps better.

After I had started this Project, I read Tessa Ransford's *Moonshine*. A short extract of her poem 'Two Halves' goes like this:

> Some like to work, some play.
>
> And some play at work
> while for others work is play
>
> *As my two half faces say.*

For me work is play, and play is often hard work; I was inspired by the way Ransford combines form and feeling, and wrote 'God Chatter' immediately after:

God Chatter

'We jump from picture to picture, and cannot follow
the living curve that is breathlessly the same' Louis MacNiece

Breathlessly the same. No dragon fire,
no wolfish pant or howl, no lion breath
to give a whiff of danger, scratch of ire;

but breathless is no euphemistic death,
no loss of grip, no lack of spark or wit,
no test of loyalty, no shibboleth;

instead it gives us God's identikit
as waiter, watcher, blowing in the air
a cloud of bubbles, what will come of it

God wonders, leaving humans with a flair
for prophecy to plunder graphic files,
or excavate another subtle layer

of Bible soil to fix in frozen piles.
Stay breathless with a God who could complete
the Ironman, then add a thousand miles,

but says, 'Been there, got the T-shirt'; so delete
that option, click on 'Do you want to see
a wave with Plato surfing on his feet

with Paul Celan?' or 'Would you rather be
an eagle with a taste for chocolate,
Benedetti in the groove, or me?'

God chattering is more than just a bit
of poetry, but taken to the wire
our world is breathless, ripe for some of it.

Postscript: My Voice

That is my voice. I hope it combines something of the following elements:

- Awe at the complexity and beauty of the cosmos
- Delight in the rhythm of words in English and Scots
- Experience of a God who is known in many ways and places
- Perception that the Psalms express ageless cries of lament and praise
- Trust in the possibility of closing the gap between the Academy and the public

Adapting the words of Eric Liddell, "when I write I feel God's pleasure".

During this book I have tried to write in a style which would appeal to those without faith as well as those more like myself. How would I now, at this stage of my life, respond to the voice of St Peter, who wrote:

> Be ready at all times to answer anyone who asks you to explain the hope you have in you, but do it with gentleness and respect.[1]

There have always been people who emphasised 'negative theology', those so aware of the immensity and unknowability of God that they prefer to talk about 'what God is not'. The poet and pastor R.S. Thomas was one of these, and his poetry appeals to many today. However I would go further.

Alexander Broadie was professor of philosophy at Glasgow, and incidentally wrote a booklet at my request which the Handsel Press published as *The Mission of Israel*. In his larger books he said there were two different approaches to Christian belief in Scotland:[2]

(a) the medieval Catholic vision, confident that the mind could work out what was good and true.

(b) the vision of Duns Scotus and the Reformers, which recognised that reason's proper function was to identify and work out a goal fixed by our own desires (as David Hume would put it later, "reason is a slave to the passions").

1 1 Peter 3:15.

2 Summarised by Professor Jim McGonigal in the book he co-edited, *Ethically Speaking: Voice and Values in Modern Scottish Writing*, Rodopi, New York 2006, page 225.

Clearly I have followed the second, in that conversion changed my desires towards loving and serving God, and it is in that context that I have had to work out what I believed. In other words, I am not just trying to think up a sensible idea of God (not that the medieval theologians would have put it like that), I am trying to respond to what has happened to me, and to what has also been the experience of believers from Abraham onwards (which the Bible records).

It has been said that God has two books, the book of nature and the book we call the Bible. In the first, we are more and more amazed by how life is complex and connected – and the view of God which seems to fit this is to see God as wonderfully involved with the process of evolution – the technical word for this is 'panentheist'.

God's other book clearly shows God to be 'personal', and at first sight these two ideas seem very different. How it is possible for God to be both?

To that I would say, as preachers have a habit of doing, three things:

First, if life is complex yet connected, is it not likely that God is even more so?

Second, Jewish and Christian thinkers have for a long time used two different words about God, transcendent and immanent, recognising that God is both far beyond us and also intimately involved with us. Poetry picks up these two ideas, without necessarily attaching 'God' to them.

Third and most important, the Bible brings the two ideas together in the person of Jesus Christ, whom John's Gospel calls 'the Word with God at the beginning'; the Greek expression for that is *logos*, which means 'reason' or 'meaning' or even 'life essence'.

It is therefore not surprising that early Christian thinkers, picking up many hints in the Bible itself, worked out the doctrine we call the Trinity. I was fortunate to be taught by T.F. Torrance at New College, one of not a few modern theologians who have taken the doctrine of the Trinity as the bedrock of Christian faith.

For the past few years I have typeset the journal of the T.F. Torrance Fellowship, *Participatio*, and helped my friend Bob Walker (nephew of Tom Torrance) with the administration of the T.F. Torrance retreats at Firbush on Loch Tay.

Although I have indicated that for me faith really came before much understanding, I am not saying the other approach is wrong. God has all kinds of ways of reaching people, and the medieval theologian Anselm wrote helpfully in *Faith Seeking Understanding* of the one leading to the other – perhaps operating like rungs of a ladder – though I wouldn't want to leave anyone thinking that we had to climb our way up to God. The heart of the gospel is that in the person of Jesus God came right down to us, to pick us up.

But if you want a ladder story, I remember once visiting the town of Safed in Israel. It hosts the Israel Bible Museum, and inside there was a beautiful sculptured impression of Jacob's ladder, with the angels going up and down as little white blobs. The important thing was the *traffic* between heaven and earth.[3] Poetry explores this traffic with the transcendent. Faith gives it a name.

I said in the Introduction that a memoir is usually a vanity project. Be that as it may, I wanted to write this as a testimony of how I have tried to respond to the opportunities of life, and behind that, how I have responded not just to what happened to me years back, but to what is happening now.

In this life and the next, there is always more, as the poet Robert Browning put it in his famous lines:

> Ah, but a man's reach should exceed his grasp,
> or what's a heaven for?[4]

---

3 The writer Francis Thompson gave this story a contemporary slant in his poem 'In No Strange Land':
> Cry; – and upon thy so sore loss
> shall shine the traffic of Jacob's ladder
> pitched between Heaven and Charing Cross.

4 From the poem 'Andrea del Sarto'.

Appendix

List of Authors of Handsel Press Booklets

Basic Studies
David Beckett, *The Lord's Supper*
William Brown, *Who are you, Holy Spirit?*
Charles Cameron, *The Bible*
Jock Stein, *Our One Baptism*
T.F. Torrance, *The Christian Doctrine of Marriage*
T.F. Torrance, *Eldership in the Reformed Church*
John Wilkinson, *Healing and the Church*
George Yule, *Mission and Unity in Christ*

Contemporary Issues
John Allan, *Dealing with Darkness*
Jeremy Begbie, *Music in God's Purposes*
Graham Bowpitt, *Social Work and Christianity*
Robert Davidson, *Christian Faith in a Nuclear Age*
Howard Davis, *The Shape of Things to Come*
Richard Frye, *Language for God*
Alasdair Heron, *Agreement and Disagreement (C of S & RC Church)*
Alan Lewis, *Theatre of the Gospel*
Mike Sheldon, *Health, Healing and Medicine*
Jock Stein, *Scottish Self-Government*
Howard Taylor, *The Delusion of Unbelief*
T.F. Torrance, *The Ministry of Women*
Andrew Thornton, *Youth Music and the Church*
Murray Watts, *Christianity and the Theatre*

Church and Israel
Alexander Broadie, *The Mission of Israel*
Samuel Lamarti Hosain, *Israel Reassessed*
Walter Riggans, *Israel and Zionism*
Howard Taylor, *World Hope in the Middle East*
David Torrance, *Mission of Christian and Jews*
David Torrance & Alastair Lamont, *Anti-Semitism and Christian Responsibility*
James Walker, *Israel – Covenant and Land*

Church Growth

Peter Bisset, *The Kirk and her Scotland*
Alec Muir, *Revivals and the Charismatic Controversy*
Lesslie Newbigin, *Mission and the Crisis of Western Culture*
Graham Smith, *In the Inner City*
Jock Stein, Ministry and Mission in the City

Tomorrow's Church (with Rutherford House)

Peter Bowes, *Children in Church Worship*
Robert Calvert & Jeremy Middleton, *From Membership to Discipleship*
Graeme Dunphy, *Celebrating Childbirth in the Church*
Robert Fyall, *Charismatic and Reformed*
Sandy Gunn, *Leadership in the Congregation*
David McAdam, *The Church and Community Involvement*
Fergus Macdonald, *The Congregation's Bible*
Peter Neilson, *Shape up for Evangelism*
David Pullinger, *The Computer in the Service of the Congregation*
Ralph Smith, *Video in the Service of the Congregation*
Jock Stein, *Singing a New Song*

Nutshell Series

Robin Barbour, *J.S. Stewart*
David Fergusson, *John Macmurray*
Joseph Houston, *Thomas Reid*
Robert Kernohan, *John Buchan*
Alan Marley, *T.F. Torrance*
James Martin, *William Barclay*
Bill Shannon, *Tom Allan*
James Torrance & Roland Walls, *John Duns Scotus*

Index of Names and Topics

Index of Poems